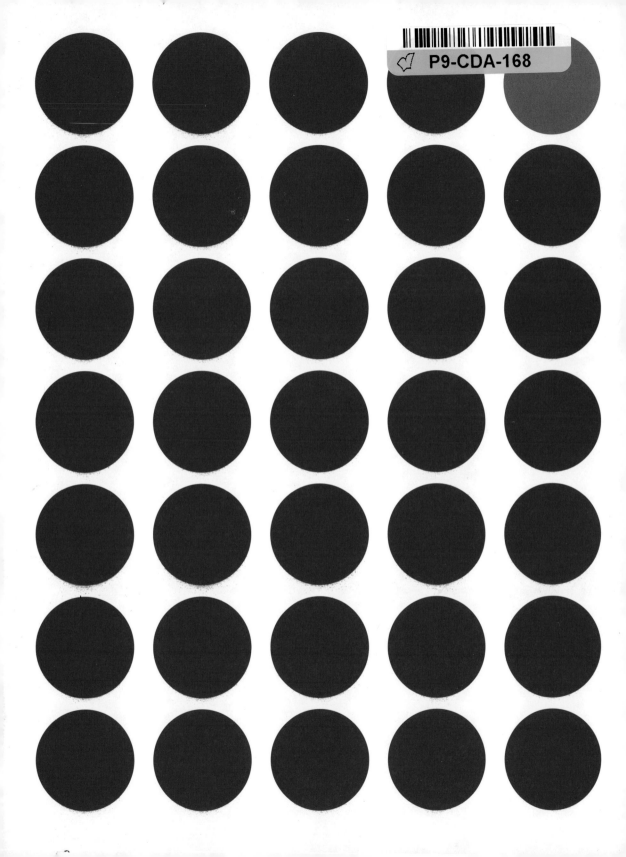

Also by Rocco DiSpirito
FLAVOR

Rocco's Italian-American

Rocco's Italian-American

ROCCO DISPIRITO & NICOLINA DISPIRITO
WITH NINA LALLI

Black & White Photography by Henry Leutwyler
Color Photography by Bill Bettencourt

HYPERION
New York

Copyright

FIRST EDITION

10 9 8 7 6 5 4 3

Acknowledgments

THANKS TO Ruba Abu-Nimah, for designing this book twice—make that three times—and still doing a great job; **all the carb lovers**, for refusing to give up pasta; **Karen Bussen,** for great work at Rocco's and her fresh approach to every project; **Scott Duncan,** for his moves, his eye, and his generosity; **American Express Small Business Network,** for putting me with the likes of **Karl Malden; David Avital,** for being my Israeli Paisano; **The Producers of The Restaurant,** especially Ben, Mark, Jaime, Roy, and Jay; **Ian Spencer Bell,** for what he doesn't say; **Bill Bettencourt,** for being cool, easy, and loving my family; **Shane Clarke,** for being all things to all people at all times; **Tolan Clark,** for rearranging the office; **David Coleman,** for his journey from UP and back, and his Svengali-like charisma; **DJ Lo,** for her Hoha-Hola; **Emily, Patty**, and **Colleen,** for managing; **Father Marchese,** for blessing my mother's meatballs; **Matthias Gaggl,** for traveling like a band of gypsies from Naples to Rome with me; **Will Grimes,** for being fair; **Jamaica, Queens,** for keeping me in the ghetto where I'm comfortable; **Kimo, Steve,** and everyone else at **Manatt, Phelps & Philips,** for finally getting this thing behind us; **Nancy Kershner,** for the best zeppole by a WASP ever; **Kristina Kurek,** for her Italian-American side; **Frank and Carole Lalli,** for their offspring; **Nina Lalli,** for being the best-dressed and for making sense of me; **Larry and Ted,** for keeping the faith; **Carla Lalli Music,** for bringing Leo into the world and still getting everything done; **Leo Lorenzo Music,** for that sparkly-eyed smile that gives one pause; **Humberto Leon,** for great uniforms; **Lateesha,** for being the best new thing in my life; **Henry Leutwyler,** for being so damn crazy and so damn talented; **Linda Lisco,** for being the smartest, the savviest, the shrewdest, and taking good care of me; **Alisha Lloyd,** for her drawl; **Mastroberadino Vineyards,** for teaming up with Antonio and Il Gastronomo to create one of the most striking and memorable lunches of my life; **Gavin McAleer**, for cooking Italian food like a Scotsman and toughing it out; **Minicuccio Restaurant** and la famiglia for their hospitality, the wood-burning stove, and for perfectly not refining Campagnan food; **Fernando Music and Fran Gaitanaros** at the Rooster Group, for my logo—I love it; **Jason Nakleh** for his golden scanning finger; **Naples,** for the Italian New York, and for those kick-ass gamberoni rossi; **Oasis Restaurant** in Vallesacrada, for their unique vision for refining Campagnan cuisine perfectly; **Parseghian Planco and Untitled,** for our home, cigars and letting us run an office like a circus—it's fun living with you; **Antonio Pisaniello,** for teaching me how to make Spaghetti Scarpariello and how to use bread-crumbs; **Fred Price,** for finally buying a new suit and for finding a place for my uncle's wine; **Saskia Rifkin,** for letting me have a crush on her; **Sandro Romano,** for his impersonation of Carla; **Lon Rosen,** for returning my phone calls; **My incredible team at William Morris,** especially Mark Itkin and Suzy Unger; **Stacey Rossley,** not for moving to LA, but for raising the bar a few notches first; **Laurent Saillard,** for being the meanest general manager I have ever seen in my life; **San Nicolo Baronia,** for my mom, my dad, the communal bakery, the wild asparagus, and for not changing too much; **Will Schwalbe,** for his good thoughts, good words, and good deeds; **Arthur Schwartz,** for knowing so much about the subject and being the Jewish guru of Southern Italian cooking; **Fred Siegal,** for his appreciation of Etro, and for being a funny-ass Jew; **Yvonne Scio,** for showing me Rome and the rest of Italy, and for being my girl during tough times; **Rob Stavis,** for his good taste, good hair, so many generous moments, and for being a stoner; **Steve, Jeff, and Paul** at Union Pacific, for nearly eight years of a groovy partnership; **Tony,** for taking care of my mom; **Jen Walsh,** for the future; **Leslie Wells,** for her amazing editing; **Uzay,** for being a celebrity waiter; **Zoie,** for being the hottest sleuth around; **Jeff and Caryn Zucker,** for their support, friendship, and TV time.

Dedication

To Anna Maria and Rocco, my grandmother and
grandfather. I knew my grandmother well, and my
grandfather only through legend. I hope this book serves
as a testament to the way they lived their lives,
and what they brought to my world.

The good life ~ every day, for everybody.

Contents

Every American

has in common the special fact that, recently or not, there was one émigré in his family who started it all by coming to America. Whether that pioneer came from Russia, Ecuador, Thailand, or Italy, her Old World values probably dictated that the family was the center of the universe, the entire social world, and the motivation for working hard. Family was also the joy in life, especially at the table. This is not an Italian phenomenon, but a human one that seems to have slipped away over the generations, especially because American families are less likely to cook dinner and sit down together for an extended period. If those people can change the way they eat, at least once a week, from just "refueling" and then disappearing to sitting down to a lengthy, relaxed meal, they would be happier and healthier. To me, the good life is lived at those tables.

In the 1950s, Americans thought that processed food was the answer to all their problems. Time was seen as so precious that shortcuts were embraced. I think we went a little too far. But, to my delight, it seems like people are starting to appreciate their ethnic backgrounds more and are rediscovering the joy of gathering around the table with their families. I think more Americans are becoming more curious about food and cooking. Even if you don't have time for a long meal during the workweek, almost every recipe in this book is simple enough to make at the end of a long day. But make it a priority to sit down for longer once a week. For my family, this is what Sundays were about. It doesn't have to be a fancy, high-maintenance menu. In fact, it shouldn't be, because the host should be able to enjoy him- or herself, and the guests should feel confident that it's OK to pick up a bone

and gnaw on it if they feel so inclined. When my mom or my aunts cook for the whole family, they put a lot of effort into the food, but not a lot of worry or stress. That's an important part of this book. Most of the recipes are either quick and easy or can be done ahead of time and then just put together right before the meal is served.

To me, there is just nothing more fulfilling and reassuring than being at the house where my grandmother lived, eating excellent food, drinking homemade wine, and laughing my ass off with my uncles, siblings, cousins, and parents. My relatives are funny, but the laughter is also a long, deep exhale of all the stress of life. When I am with them, I can really feel, physically even, the letting go of a lot of that stress. The feeling of barriers coming down, of forgetting the concerns of how to act and what one should say, of truly relaxing, is such a good feeling, I can't help but lean back and laugh. It's restorative. I've been lucky enough to meet famous people, travel all over the world, and be on TV, but I think people who don't experience the warmth of sitting at a table for a few hours, eating home-cooked food, and being with people they love and who love them are really missing out.

This feeling can come from good friends, which are often "family" to us. (As a kid, I had a lot of extra "uncles.") It can be a celebration of ancestry and the fact that, as Americans, we have the opportunity to share other cultures and food. So if you're Russian, Ecuadorian, or Thai, this book is a way to take a piece of the good life from me and make it part of you. Something happens in the middle of a table, between people, when they eat together. It's not ultimately about the food, but when you're eating good food, you do feel better and happier. It's not about the way the table settings look, although seeing beautiful flowers is pleasing. All these sensual experiences play supporting or facilitating roles to that of the conversations, the looks, laughter, and the celebration of one another.

If this kind of eating is part of your life, you can probably conjure vivid memories when you think about certain food. For me, it's meatballs, frittata, sausages, and homemade pasta. I want to share it with everyone. I opened my restaurant, Rocco's 22nd Street, as an homage to my family and an invitation to all New Yorkers and Americans to be part of it through eating the food. This book will give you the other side of the experience: the cooking, and the freedom to make the good life part of your life and your family. I am an experienced chef who knows all the fancy techniques and exotic ingredients and all that. But it all means nothing unless it is applied to what really matters in life.

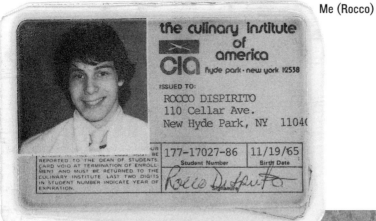

Me (Rocco)

My dad, Rafaelle

Uncle Joe &
Zia Elena

Uncle Silvio & Zia Maria

Mama (my mom, Nicolina)

My sister Maria

My brother Michael

Cast *of* Characters

For all their inspiration, recipes, high standards, guidance, and love I would like to express my gratitude to my family and paisani: my grandmother, Anna Maria Iaccoviello; my grandfather, Rocco; my mother; my father; my sister Maria; Jack; Mike; Andrew; my brother Michael; Patty; Brooke; Michael; Uncle Amadeo; Nina; Mario; Mario; Rocco; Uncle Davide and all his family in Germany; Uncle Silvio and Zia Maria; Angela; Anna; Rocco; Michelle; Lauren; Julia; Uncle Joe and Zia Elena; Anna Maria; Josephine; Godmother Margarita and Alfonso; Camilla and Tommy; Lisa and Crista; the Morgans; the Lazzarollos; Angelina Gasparini; Nicky; Ronnie; Patty; Laura; Patty, Gino, and their family: Lella, Joey, Angela, Isadore; Concettina; Giuseppina; Emanuela; Raffiellina; Pasqualina; Vincenzina; and all the other hangers-on, droppers-by, good eaters, those who helped make wine and drink it, who baked bread and shared it.

Nicolina's Story

One of my earliest memories is being up very late with my three little brothers (the fourth, Silvio, was still to come), when I was about seven. We weren't resisting our parents' efforts to get us to sleep; it was the opposite. My father, the first Rocco, wouldn't let us go to bed! It was the night before the biggest holiday, Christmas Eve. My mother was in the kitchen making baccalà, and my father gathered all four of us kids in his outstretched arms. We all stood in the doorway of the kitchen, me and my brothers all around and between my father's long legs. He said to us: "Watch what your mother does, very carefully, and learn from her!" And we did, with fascination. To us it seemed like magic, absolute magic, that she could make perfect, delicious food out of practically nothing.

We had very little, and yet she could create nourishment that was full of flavor and warmth. My brothers, Davide, Giuseppe, Amadeo, and Silvio, and I would marvel at the things she made, saying, "Mama made this, Mama made that!" bragging about her to one another. We could hardly believe our eyes. My father clearly thought it was magical, too. We could tell that he deeply respected her talent and thought it was important work. It was a beautiful thing, to show us kids that, and I can never forget it. I hope I taught my children the same respect for food and family.

We didn't have a fancy stove. We cooked over a fire in the kitchen. Well, we didn't really have a kitchen. Our house had two rooms. One was the bedroom. In the corner of the other room was a fire pit with a three-legged stand above it, where we put pots for cooking, and there was a table where we ate. That was the kitchen. But still, she could do anything. I am from a town called San Nicolo Baronia, which at the time had a population of six hundred, mostly struggling families just like us. We knew each other like a book in that town. We shared values and traditions. It is near Avellino and about a two hours' drive from Naples.

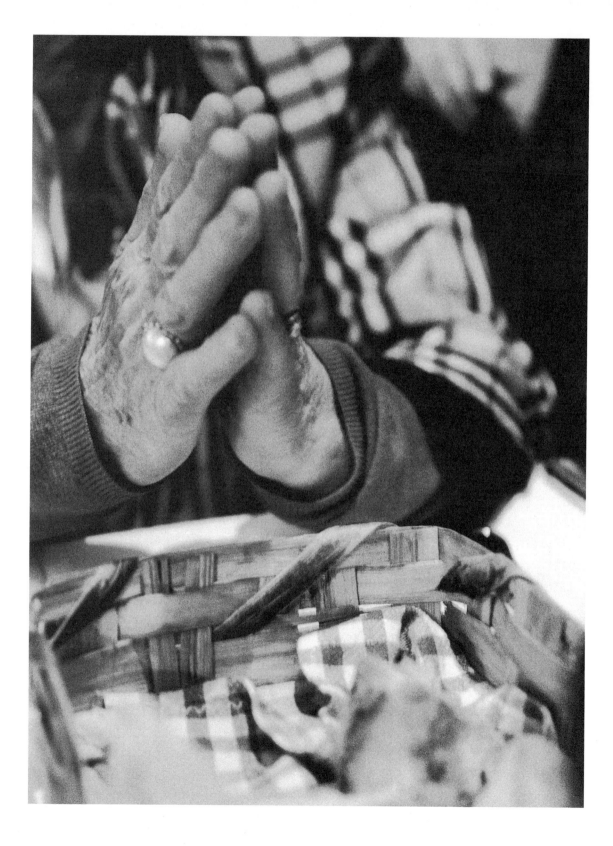

Part of the magic of our kitchen, when I was young, was the way my mother made the work fun. She would do silly things with extra bits of dough if she was baking, like make a little doggie for us. Even when I was young, cooking wasn't only about how good everything tasted when it got to the table. The fun was in the process, the time together in the kitchen. When you cooked with Mama, you felt proud, and dinner tasted even better than usual. It's necessary to experience that. Even though we often didn't have much to eat, a lot of my happiest memories, especially those about my parents, are related to food. So for me to cook, it's a lot more than just making dinner.

Food, to me, is really about love. When I was young, my father used to go out at night and play cards, and, hopefully, he would win. But the men didn't bet money, because no one had any. So if he won, he won a piece of cheese. I remember it so well, this picture is right in the front of my head: he would break the cheese into pieces and first, he would give one to my mother, his wife. He would put it right in her mouth, and then my brothers and I would come around him and he would do the same thing for us. It looked like we were a family of little birdies being fed. My father could have just eaten the cheese himself. He was hungry, I know that. But he did not do that. We shared everything.

I have wonderful memories, thanks to my mother and father. Wonderful, wonderful, wonderful. And it's amazing, because my childhood was very tragic. I think parents can give their children happy memories no matter how much pain they might go through in life. We were very poor in Italy, and there are many things about my past that make me sad, but I can't forget what was good. I think the good stuff made me and my brothers realize there was hope in trying to make a new life—that it was worth it to try. It gave us a little glimpse of happiness, a place that would be about positive things.

In 1930, I was six years old. One day, my parents had to spend the whole day working in the church. When they came home, I knew they would be starving and I felt bad for them. So I had a little yellow flour. I made the fire and brought some water to a boil in a little black kettle. Then I put the cornmeal in, and I was stirring and stirring it. You have to stir continuously, but I did not, because my arms got so tired, so the smoke came up, *bloop bloop*, and the polenta was burned. Here, you could throw it out and start over, but that thought would never come into my head then; that was all we had. My mother put it in a bowl, and I gave it to my father, who ate the entire thing, every bite. I knew it was burned; he knew it was terrible; but he said it was the best polenta he'd ever had in his whole life.

When I was about ten years old, Mussolini came into power, and the government wanted to give my family 500 lire, a stipend for the poor, which was a lot of money then, especially to people like us. My father turned down the charity. He said he wanted a job instead, the opportunity to earn his own money. That's when he got a job in North Africa doing manual labor. When he left, my mother was pregnant with my youngest brother, Silvio. Two years later, without coming back for a break, my father died. He dropped his hat, went to reach for it, and was hit by a truck. He was thirty-three years old; I was twelve. That's a story I don't

even want to tell; it's very painful to think about. I loved my father very, very much.

My life changed drastically. I was devastated; we all were. On top of the sadness of losing him, our lives got harder after he was gone. My mother had to work, and I had to raise my four little brothers. My mother had no choice but to leave us to work; we had to eat. But she left me with four little brothers! I did the best I could. That's not easy for a twelve-year-old. My mother worked anywhere, whatever she could find—a day here, a day there. It wasn't like in America, where you can usually find something, even if it's something no one else would want to do. It was very different where we lived. We had no welfare, no help at all. She was the most wonderful mother any kid could have.

I was twenty-four years old when I came to America. I came because I wanted a better life. For me, for my brothers, for my mother—everybody. I was the first one to do it, and when I came, it was for my family. I made about seventy cents an hour at my first job, and I never spent even a penny, because I wanted to send it to my mother. I could not go to the movies, because my mother was starving. I couldn't do it. I knew she did not have anything.

I flew to New York, where I had an uncle Tony who had a dry cleaning and alterations business. He was really the friend of my uncle in Italy, but we call everyone "Uncle." He wasn't related to me, but he was like family. We call that "famiglietti." The day I arrived, I went there directly from the airport and worked for nine hours. I was a dressmaker there for three years. I wasn't bad, either. I stayed with my uncle in Queens. At their house, I ate pretty much the same food as I had in Italy; I remember a lot of pasta and beans. No one could cook like my Mama, but I was very grateful that my uncle's family took care of me all that time. It was a wonderful thing they did. I would have eaten anything!

After those three years, I went back to Italy to marry my husband, Rafaelle. I had known him my entire life. But it wasn't like in America, where you're boyfriend and girl-friend before getting engaged. There's no such thing in Italy, and especially then; you

were either "friend" or "fiancé." There's no word for "boyfriend" in Italian. I stayed in Italy for two weeks, and when I came back to New York, I was pregnant with my daughter, Maria. Raf wasn't able to move to America then because of his health. When he took his examination, the doctors found a spot on his lung that was probably tuberculosis. They kept him in Italy and monitored him for almost four years before they let him come here. So, when I returned to New York, I was twenty-seven years old, married, pregnant, and alone. When Maria was born, in 1955, God gave me the best gift of my life. She was my friend. She was everything to me. We were alone together.

I moved to Jamaica, Queens, where I stayed until 1980. I worked in a blouse factory in the neighborhood the whole time I was pregnant, but I got a better job in a sweater factory after Maria was born. I made seventy-five cents per dozen sweaters. I was a fast worker, and I could make five dozen an hour. It was very hard for me to leave Maria at home, because I had painful memories of being left when my own mother had to work. But I had no choice, just like my mother. I learned to be independent, and to take care of myself and my child, but I feel sad just thinking about leaving her. At least I had a wonderful friend who took care of Maria when I was gone.

I got a night job, too, in a toy factory, I always had two jobs, nearly all my life! Wherever I could find work, I did it. This is serious stuff: when you have nothing, you cannot be choosy. Not at all. I'm just one person, but I had to be more, like everyone who comes here alone. Jamaica was nice back then. It was beautiful. I was never scared to walk home, even late at night. There were almost no Italians in the neighborhood, at least not near us. I had Jewish friends. I met a lot of wonderful people with different backgrounds, and that was something new for me. That's New York. That's America. I struggled, but I always loved it here. I knew I was going toward a better and better life.

I called my brothers and my mother and told them to come here, too. In 1957, when I was thirty-one years old and Maria was almost three, my mother and Rafaelle came to America. Finally, I could really see the better life I had imagined starting to take shape. I had support because I had my family again.

Once Raf was here, I didn't work until Rocco, the baby, was in first grade. That's about twelve years, and after that I only worked part-time. It was a goal I had to achieve, a promise I made to myself, to be with my kids. That was a luxury to me. We could barely afford it, but I chose to have a little less and be able to be home with my kids. Anyway, I think the more money you make, the more

you'll spend. This dream had started for me from the experiences I had, of being a kid left alone and of being a mother who had to work and had no choice but to be away from her baby. Goals usually happen in small steps, and I think I accomplished a lot.

In the very beginning, we all lived together—my mother, Rafaelle, and me. Rafaelle was a cabinetmaker. When he first arrived, I worked until he found work. My mother stayed home with Maria, and she was so excited to spend time with her granddaughter because she had not been there when she was born. Then Mama got married and moved into a beautiful house in West Hempstead, Long Island, with her husband, who was a very good man. The way she lived in Long Island was just like in Italy, but better. She had a bigger house and more land, and she used it. She had rabbits, pigeons, chickens, and every kind of vegetable and fruit you can think of: fig trees, lemon trees, everything. She made unbelievable dinners. She loved to work in the garden almost as much as she loved to cook. Everything she planted grew up nicely. Me, everything I plant, it dies. I don't know what it is. Well, at least I can cook.

My brother Giuseppe lived in the house with her, with his wife, Elena, and their two daughters, Anna Maria and Josephine. It made me happy to have her here, and I was

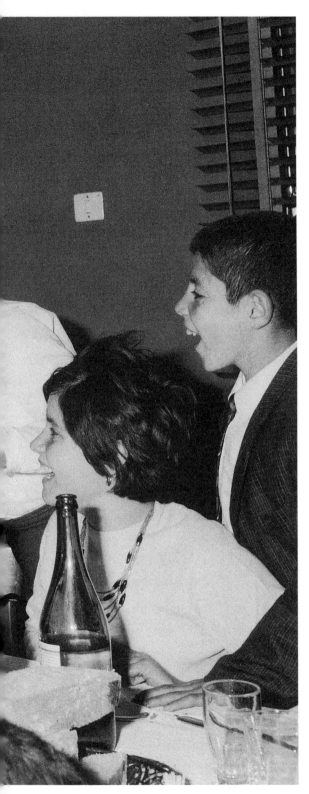

glad that Joe lived with her. She had been alone so much in her life, widowed at twenty-six. It was never easy. When I became a mother myself, I really understood all about it, how hard her life had been and what a strong and wonderful person she was. Mothers, especially the poor ones, make a lot of sacrifices, all for their kids. We do without a lot of things, a lot of experiences, and we don't even consider another option, if it means our kids will get to go to college and become the people they want to be.

She was tiny, even smaller than I am. She wasn't even five feet tall. She was adorable. Everybody who knew her loved my mother. She was never selfish; she was wise, and she made everyone around her feel great. She hated gossip. If someone came in her house and started to talk about someone else's business, she would say, "I don't wanna know about that! Let's have a coffee!" She said that all the time, just changed the subject and kept feeding us. It worked.

We were always at her house, me and my brothers. As the family in New York got bigger, she was always the center of everything; her house was the family meeting place. Every Sunday, we were all there for the whole day. We spent the most beautiful Christmases with her there. Since she died in 1992, it's not the same. She made everything right. You know, if I was angry at one of my brothers, I didn't care, because I loved my mother. To sit down at her table, especially on a holiday, it made everything great, just like that. If I hadn't been at her house, I didn't feel right after a few days. My kids missed her if we didn't see her all the time. We had to go! I was very glad for that, because I know that some kids don't want to go see Grandma or Grandpa; they say, "They're too old," "they're no fun"—all that baloney.

I think my father would have loved to see the way Rocco paid attention when I was cooking, like he told us to do when we were young. I cooked with Maria and Michael, but I could tell Rocco had a deeper interest in food. He was very curious all the time. I always cooked the way my mother had, and I taught him what I knew, too. Mostly, I think he just took it in from being with me. With kids, the most important thing, the first thing, is to watch.

When Rocco got to be about six, I started working part-time in an executive cafeteria in Manhattan. We made lunch for ten or twelve big-shot people, but they were wonderful people. It made me much happier to be working with food than in a factory like before. I cannot write English. I cannot write Italian. I can't do anything except cook, and I can't really explain why, but it makes me happy to work with food. It's a kind of therapy. I don't know why people spend so much money on the psychiatrist! Not everybody has that feeling about cooking, I know, but I think everyone feels better being in a kitchen or at the table eating good food.

Anyway, I would go to work after I dropped Rocco off at school, and I would be home when he got back, because as soon as he was in the door, he'd be yelling, "Maaaaaama!" I had to be there. He was a good kid, and a happy kid. We always cooked at home; we almost never went to restaurants, we never went to the movies, we never did anything. We just had what we needed. And it was good, too.

We moved to New Hyde Park in 1980. I got a job at a deli near our new house. And soon after that, I also got a job working in the cafeteria at the public school back in Jamaica. I took the bus back and forth all week. I loved working with kids. I loved that job. I worked at the deli part-time and I loved that, too. At both places, I got a lot of experience making all kinds of food: tuna salad, chicken salad, rice, macaroni, spaghetti. Whatever they needed, I made it. When you go to work and there's a job to do, you do it. I didn't want to force my own recipes and dishes on anyone, but I made some of my specialties, like meatballs and lasagna. I worked at the deli until I started working with Rocco at his restaurant.

I worked at the school for twenty years. My boss was a Puerto Rican lady who was wonderful. I love her very much, and she loves me, too. I think working at the school was my favorite job. But I loved the deli, too. You know, if you like to work, any job you have, you're going to figure out how to make the best of it. If you don't like to work, you'll hate it everywhere you go, and then you have big problems!

Working at Rocco's restaurant, it's like I'm born again into a new life. I never could have expected anything like this happening to me. I love it. It makes me happier than anything. I really feel like I have a new life to live. I love cooking with all the great guys downstairs in the kitchen, and I love seeing the people who come in to eat. I like to make the people happy, talk to them, and see them having a good time and great food. I feel proud, and honestly, happier than I've ever been.

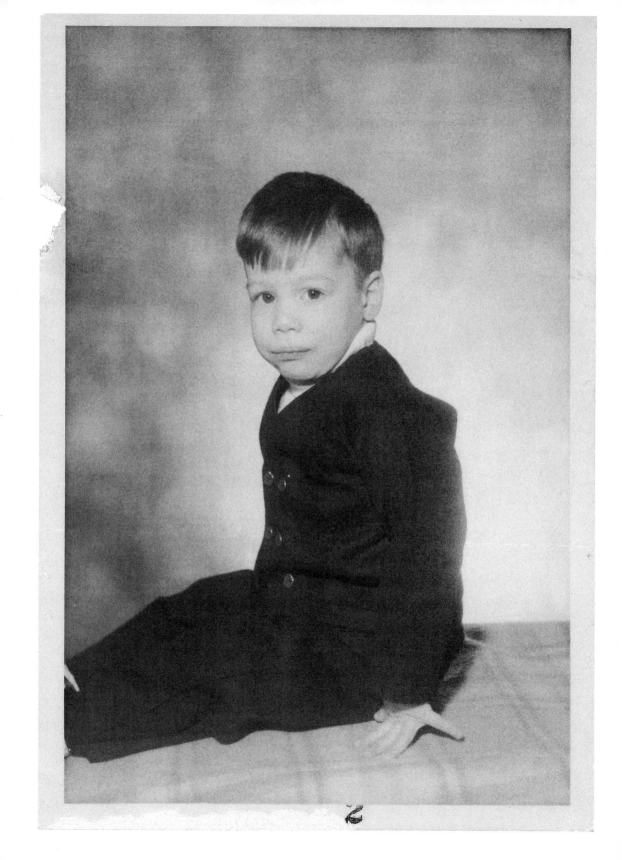

Rocco's Story

My school lunch was the earliest sign to me that I was different from other kids. I'd have a few pieces of my mom's homemade Italian bread with some soppressata my uncle made and a hunk of provolone cheese; there was also an apple or a banana for dessert. It was packed in a rumpled, grease-stained (reused) brown paper bag. Nothing inside was individually wrapped. My mom certainly did not worry about plastic wrap and Tupperware. As I remember it, every single one of my classmates had peanut butter and jelly on spongy Wonder Bread with the crusts cut off, neatly wrapped in tight plastic with a juice box and, for dessert, Twinkies, Yodels, or individual pudding cups. They gawked at my thick slices of crusty bread and chunk of cheese like I was an alien imposter. I felt like maybe I was.

When I was eating my mom's frittatas, they were eating American cheese omelets; when I was eating my uncle Joe's homemade cappicola, they were eating Oscar Mayer bologna; when I was eating my aunt Elena's handmade pasta with marinara sauce made from tomatoes my grandmother grew in her garden, they were eating slimy canned SpaghettiOs. Looking back, I feel lucky, even superior. But back then, I was mortified.

I grew up in an ethnic neighborhood in Queens called Jamaica. Many of the kids in my Catholic school were African-American and Latino. The rest were white and nonethnically oriented, like third-generation Irish-American kids, who, to me, were simply white. This was not an Italian enclave where a whole village had seemingly been transplanted across the Atlantic Ocean, life simply continuing on but with bigger cars. I didn't have any Italian friends. I was different and I felt it, especially at school, where the differences seemed magnified. It wasn't just my lunch. But that was my earliest and most poignant memory of feeling vulgar and peasant-like.

Recently, the label *artisanal* has become a major status symbol for foodies. Artisanal means handmade by artisans and usually refers to bread, cheese, and pasta. It has become chic to prefer artisanal food, which is considered very special and superior—and it is! But now handmade food is "fancy"; a lot of Americans grew up in a world of processed, mass-produced, and frozen foods, so what peasants once did in the villages of Italy is exotic to them. They are also starting to insist on organic vegetables and to scorn preservatives. Little did I know that I grew up eating an incredibly fashionable artisanal diet in Queens. The craft of cooking was, in Italy, a cornerstone; like any trade, it was, and still is, valued and handed down to each generation with pride. But that craft was simultaneously taken for granted. Making pasta by hand wasn't a special skill; it was simply the way women made pasta. My grandmother, mother, and aunts made everything by hand, grew what they could, and didn't think twice about it. They didn't call it "artigionale" because there was no other version of things. Perhaps if I had known how posh my school lunches would become, I would have bragged about them, rather than hiding the paper bags in my cubby.

My parents were both born in a poor village called San Nicolo Baronia, in Campagna. Like most immigrants, they both struggled significantly in their youth in Italy as well as after they arrived in New York. When they came here, in the 1950s, their traditions were not carried

out as deliberate efforts to hold on to the past; they were just how they did things. I don't think my parents, or at least my mother, felt that old methods of cooking or doing anything else were threatened to change in a new setting. The culture in Italy, especially when my parents were growing up, assumed that everyone had a little plot of land where he raised some livestock, everyone made his own wine and baked his own bread. And when my grandmother got here, she didn't change a thing. Why would she?

In the Augusts of my childhood, my parents and I used to take the bus to Nonna's (Grandma's) house every Sunday around noon, as we did all year round. But in August, there was a particular seduction in the visits: it was fig season. My grandmother, who was not much taller than I was then, would appear in front of the house to greet me, always with a little basket made of fig leaves and filled with the ripest figs, gathered from her trees and the ground. She handed it to me with both hands outstretched. I could smell them before they were in my hands—before I could even see them. I will never forget that welcome. It remains one of the best feelings I've ever had, seeing her standing there with the figs, just for me, because she knew I loved them.

My sister, Maria, has similar memories; she was a picky eater as a kid. One of the few things she really loved was angel-hair pasta with butter. Angel-hair was almost never to be found in my mother's house, because my father liked only linguine, so Nonna would make that special just for her, without her asking, while we all ate something else. When I think about my family and my childhood, I think about figs and all the activity around those trees. But more than any particular food, what we all remember is a feeling of the good life, a constant celebration of just being together.

I have learned from the immigrants in my family that the American Dream is defined on an individual basis. My grandmother Anna Maria Iacoviello realized hers in the form of an almost self-sufficient farm paradise in West Hempstead, Long Island. She came to New York in 1957, six years after my mother moved here, and bought her house a few years after that, when she married a sweet old Italian man we called Uncle Charlie, whom she met here. To me, then and now, her house was a magical place, a piece of Italian soil in New York. To her mind, the house was nice—a good house. The way it functioned was what any reasonable person would want: an effective irrigation system, a year-round rotation of fruits and vegetables, room for chickens, rabbits, and so on. She simply set up a civilized household in the expected manner—keeping the animals and growing the vegetables she needed. This was practical; this was the only way to live, in her eyes. For most Americans, it's hard to imagine planting every vegetable you need rather than running to the store for them. Before I started school, I assumed everyone's grandmother was an Italian farmer like mine.

The house was like the one in which my mother and uncles were raised in San Nicolo Baronia, but with one major improvement: more space, inside and outside. Nonna had land. Today, three houses stand on that plot. My uncle Joe lives there still, with his wife, Elena. Nonna had chickens, pheasants, and pigeons, and occasionally, a live pig would be brought to her house for its final hours before Uncle Joe, a butcher, slaughtered it for a barbecue. There was a black fig tree, a white fig tree, a cherry tree, a variety of apple trees, a pear tree, a compost heap (which I can still picture with its animal parts and decomposing grass). She had blackberry trees, and what she called *civere*, which just means "cherries"; they were similar to boysenberries, but better. The berries were white, red, and black and grew on tall branches. I obsessed over them, they were so good. Uncle Joe used to climb the trees and shake the limbs, and my siblings and cousins and I held an old bedsheet below to catch the berries. She also grew a few kinds of lettuces, like escarole, arugula, and romaine, red and white onions, broccoli, carrots, rutabagas, parsley, basil, tomatoes, green bell peppers, Cubanelle peppers, chili peppers, zucchini, eggplants, cucumbers, garlic, cabbages, cauliflower, peas, apricots, grapes, peaches, plums, sour and sweet cherries, and more. Everywhere you looked, something was growing. She rarely went to ShopRite. So we ate according to season, which is another recent gastronomic trend in this country, where one can have avocados every day. But we also always preserved certain things like tomatoes and peppers in the summer and fall, so we could eat them in the winter.

For my family, my grandmother's home was always a sanctuary. My mother and grandmother made it a restorative place for the family. The word *restaurant* comes from the word *restaurare*, which means "to restore." It originally referred to gathering around the table at home with one's family and later came to describe hospitality. My grandmother's house was a working farm, but she loved the work so much that she blurred the worlds we tend to think of as separate: living and working. Everything had a purpose but was, at the same time, comfortable and calm. For example, the grapes grew on an arched trellis, which created a shady sitting area, which was the dreamiest place to sleep in the afternoon. My nonna would make me take a nap there when I was young.

That farm was our paradise. It wasn't luxurious. Everything had a little bit of dirt on it or was a little banged up. No one cared, though. My grandmother was a deeply satisfied person. Though she had suffered greatly earlier in life, or maybe because she knew what it was to suffer, she appreciated her new life consciously. Spending time with her children and

grandchildren, watching each generation struggle a little less, and being able to work and live on her own terms were huge successes and sources of satisfaction. We were lucky to share the best part of her life with her.

Nonna's house had three kitchens. There was a small kitchen on the top floor, near her bedroom, that was never used until she was very old and kept a few things in there, like a tea kettle. Then there was the "upstairs kitchen" on the ground floor, which had been renovated to high standards. There were marble counters, nice cabinets, and new appliances. We never used that kitchen, either. That one had to look good. The work was done in the converted basement. This is the way it is in many rural houses I've visited in Italy—it is common to have a "show" kitchen, while the real work takes place hidden away where you would think the car is parked (and sometimes is, right next to a long table). I never understood the point of the show kitchen when I was a kid. Especially because, 99 percent of the time, it was only the family who came over, and we were always in the basement kitchen with her. So who was she trying to impress?

Her cooking was a different story, of course. That always impressed me. As a kid, it seemed like she and my mother and aunt had special powers over food. They never messed up, never burned anything, and never came across some food they didn't know what to do with. They had all the answers and they hardly talked about what they were doing as they did it. They moved swiftly, surely, and gracefully. I'm still impressed. There was no wishy-washy food in my mother's house, either. There was nothing bland, no overcooked vegetables or watery sauces. At the same time, things were never overseasoned or greasy. Nothing was ever haphazard; even if it was thrown together at the last minute, it was amazing. I learned that it was not a supernatural power, it was not memorization of recipes and techniques; the food was so good because they knew how it should taste and feel, and they tasted it often.

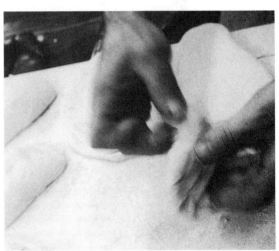

Every Sunday, an enormous feast was orchestrated for the entire family. We kids were all expected to dress up nicely for church and go straight to Nonna's from there. Supper was served by about one o'clock. She had a long table made of sawhorses and plywood, to which she had stapled a red-and-white checkered tablecloth and covered the whole thing with clear plastic. For special occasions, she would cover that with a white cotton tablecloth, but generally she did not.

On Sundays, there were always twenty to thirty people at her house for about ten hours. If anyone had ever cut the visit short, on either end, it would have been considered scandalously rude. I don't think that ever happened. The bulk of those hours was occupied by cooking and eating. But the men also played bocce and a card game, scopa, which means "broom." I never learned how to play; I was too busy running around in the yard with my cousins, getting in trouble. I'd steal my uncle's guns and try to shoot birds out of the sky.

The entire repertoire of my family probably consists of about one hundred savory dishes, which we ate again and again. The recipes were not written down or officially passed down at any point. They were woven deeply into our way of life. The Sunday menu featured all the favorites. First there were antipasti. The big table was filled with different dishes: homemade bread, homemade soppressata, Joe's specialty, as was the red wine we drank, though the women and kids mixed in soda.

Then came the primo, or the pasta course. There was always a special pasta—the most labor-intensive ones, like manicotti, lasagna, and ravioli, were considered special. Also, the thinnest long pastas were special—like spaghettini and angel-hair, perhaps because they, too, were difficult to handle. The pasta sauce was ragù or "gravy"—marinara sauce in which several types of meat had been braised all day. We ate the meat separately, a tradition from Southern Italy. Over time, in Italian-American restaurants, that gave way to pasta as a side order with meat.

After the primo was, of course, secondo, which generally could be meat or fish; on Sundays it is always meat, mainly the meat that had cooked in the ragù: braciola, sausage, and meatballs. We also had roasted quail or chicken cacciatora, sometimes pheasants, rabbit cacciatora, or roasted rabbit and potatoes.

After that, we always had dessert, though this was the course we focused on least. Rich, heavy desserts were never part of my life until I went to France in my late teens. Often "dolce" was just fruit, but biscotti became a staple when I was a teenager. My aunt Maria, the baker in the family, developed an excellent biscotti recipe (see page 230), which is a great example of the family's Americanizing; hers are much softer than the traditional biscotti, which are meant for dipping in coffee or grappa. Ours also have chocolate chips, whereas Italian biscotti usually are plain or have hazelnuts. On many Sundays, my aunt Elena made her famous Ricotta Grain Cake (see page 234). And, of course, there was always fresh fruit and nuts and cordials, coffee, anisette.

Cooking and eating were easy, natural, and instinctive ways of expressing love, in my grandmother's house and in my mother's. Although my parents had some fundamental differences, and my father was the "head of the household," my mother made sure our house was a place where we all felt good: revived, nurtured, and loved. As the stereotypical Italian mother is

always depicted, a moment did not go by when my mom wasn't cooking or offering us something to eat. But it never seemed silly to me; that gesture was the most warm, maternal thing I could imagine. It was her absolute expression of love and one of her only ways of fulfilling her life's destiny, which, as she saw it, was to take care of other people.

She had overcome monumental challenges for us. She came here alone and really built our family, struggling for years so she could eventually provide this sanctuary for us. The main definition of the sanctuary was having plenty of good food to eat. Food was the one and only thing my parents were willing to splurge on. We never went on vacation, we always wore hand-me-downs and often played with makeshift toys, but we had more than enough food to eat all the time. To my mother, this was the American Dream: to be able to raise children who did not have to struggle unduly, who had plenty to eat, and who could go to school and create their own dreams. These ideals were based on what she had missed in her own childhood in Italy.

Neither of my parents went to school past the fourth grade. This was one of their greatest sacrifices for their parents. My father's family had slightly more money than my mother's, but for both of them, at a very young age, work took precedence over school. My father studied through high school on his own and got a high school degree in New York. He always fancied himself an intellectual, someone who might pass the day sitting in cafés talking about politics. His goal was to become a lawyer. But when he got here, he quickly realized that life was about working twelve hours a day, six days a week, getting overtime, and struggling for his wife and children. For him, the streets were not paved with gold because the struggle had not ended. For my mother, and many immigrants, the "gold" was being able to find work, to have the chance to make a better life, not so much for themselves as for the next generation.

That is the distinct difference between them. My mother feels that the American Dream came true for her, while my father feels personally disappointed. It is evident in how they talk about Italy. My father wonders whether life might have ultimately been better for him had he stayed where he was. And my mother is sure it would have been a lot worse. She has actually said she hates Italy because of the losses she suffered there.

As a kid, I moved within a wide cultural landscape, despite the fact that my parents both came from an impoverished village of six hundred people. My parents were very open to the new people and different cultures that were unavoidable in Queens. There are more countries (over 150) represented and languages (over 100) spoken in Queens than in any place in the world. My mom was open-minded and openhearted; she embraced everything America had to offer. This mostly came in the form of indulging my favorite pastime: explorative eating. She would go anywhere I wanted, to any borough, to try any kind of food. My father tried his best to acculturate. He learned English, got his high school diploma here, read *The New York Times* every day, and got into politics. He never became an American citizen, but he directs the voting in our house. It's pretty funny, really, because my mom will vehemently argue his opinions without really knowing why.

My parents had totally different ways of adapting to life here. For my mom, it was about being out in the world, making different kinds of friends, and being part of the community. Her accent even changed as I got older; it became more of a Queens accent than the heavy Italian twang she had once had. She even learned all the curse words when she worked in the cafeteria at PS 79 in Jamaica. For my father, it was much more of an internal process, more of a philosophical pondering and observing. My mom knows what she knows and is wise from experience.

Even though we mainly realized our Italian identity through food, which was my mother's

realm, it was my father who thought and talked about those things in terms of conscious preservation. My father talked about keeping traditions alive, but my mother "made it happen," to use kitchen parlance. At least that's how I thought of it, but by watching her cook, unbeknownst to me, I was training and developing my palate. I realized that as soon as I got to culinary school. Those afternoons with Mom were an incredibly valuable education. My mother always encouraged me to cook, and there was also plenty of trial and error involved. In my early teens, she worked until five or six at night, so my brother and I would have to fend for ourselves in the kitchen. All my brother, Michael, ever wanted to eat was forbidden things, like Weaver frozen chicken and all that processed food; I, too, used to beg for Swanson frozen TV dinners. Turkey and Salisbury steak were my favorites.

My mom occasionally snuck off with me to McDonald's, which I loved; it was really my dad who was strict about this. But my curiosity about new flavors led me more often toward ethnic

cuisines than Big Macs. The older I got, the more I craved food I had never tasted before—certainly not the typical lust of an adolescent boy. I loved food, thanks to my family, and I wanted to taste everything the rest of the world's kitchens had to offer.

While I was growing up in Jamaica, right outside our front door was an incredibly diverse world; there was a huge Latin-American population (from several countries), African-American, Irish, German, Jewish, Chinese, Indian, Pakistani, Greek, Jamaican, West Indian, and so forth. So there were all these different kinds of food to taste. When I was eleven years old, I got a job, my first of three summer jobs at pizzerias. I saved my money, and my mom would take me shopping for all sorts of exotic food. It was an adventure, all the time. My neighborhood has been an enormous inspiration to me as a chef. I developed the fundamental relationship with food and cooking at my grandmother's table and in my mother's kitchen; then I began to study all the possibilities of flavor by eating in my neighborhood.

I had no idea, at the time, what a positive influence Jamaica would be on my life. In fact, I hated it when I lived there. It was a tough neighborhood, I got mugged constantly, our house was burglarized—it was your classic crime-ridden ghetto. And it got increasingly worse until we moved to Long Island in 1980, when I was fourteen. It had been a working-class neighborhood since the 1920s, and then in 1976, when I was ten, the government started a federally funded courthouse project that required the clearing out of several middle-income apartment buildings. They were going to be demolished in order to build the courthouse, but the project was abandoned and the empty buildings became low-income housing. The neighborhood changed very drastically, very suddenly, and very much for the worse.

Our house was situated on the cusp between a big Latino area, which had formerly been a Greek neighborhood, like Astoria still is, and an African-American neighborhood. Our Greek neighbors used to steal the dandelions that grew outside our front door (see page 199). Greeks owned and ran most of the restaurants and shops on the Latino side, so all the diners were Greek. We ate souvlaki at those places. The pizzerias were also owned by Greeks, for the most part, and the menus were Italian and Greek. The blocks surrounding us were mostly made up of apartment buildings; our block was a lone strip of houses, which by contrast was somewhat upscale.

Most of the Latin-American kids in my neighborhood were not ashamed at all of who they were. They celebrated their heritage every day. And I joined in, especially with my

snobby, especially to me and my parents, because they thought they were better Italians. At the same time, my cousins felt a little superior because they lived on Long Island. Most of them had started out in our neighborhood and moved on when they were young. I was a city kid, and by the time they were teenagers, they were basically convinced that the five boroughs consisted solely and abundantly of gang violence, drug shoot-outs, and sexual deviance.

Although my mom indulged my addiction to international snacking after school, going out to dinner was not a frequent experience for our family. Unlike most Americans, my family did not yearn to eat dinner in fancy places, or out anywhere for that matter. When we did go to a restaurant for a special occasion, it was almost always an Italian restaurant owned by a friend of a friend who came from the same town as my parents (so it was as similar to being at a relative's house as possible). The exception was a Chinese take-out place in the neighborhood. It was tacky, with booths and lots of Formica. A Chinese couple owned it. The husband was the manager and ran the delivery operation, which was the first thing you saw when you entered. His wife was in charge of the kitchen. I was in love with her. Although she was a cook, she always wore a long black robe, never an apron or a chef's jacket. She

best friend, Robert Ruiz, who was Ecuadorean. I loved spending time with his family, especially in the kitchen with his mother, who taught me how to make ceviche. That became the basis of many recipes I created at Union Pacific. Even though things didn't look the way they did at my house, or sound and taste the same, we had in common the most basic things. Robert's parents worked hard for the family, ate the way they had in their native country, and joined together with their relatives over food. That was the main point, to be together as a family.

Unlike Robert, and other Latin-Americans I knew growing up, I was self-conscious about my ethnicity, largely because I hardly knew any Italians I wasn't related to. I did go to school with one Italian boy who lived in a better part of Queens. But his family was

was beautiful. She had perfect skin, blue-black hair in a bun, and she smiled broadly and warmly, unlike her husband, who was a pathetic figure. He was a stereotypical Chinese restaurant owner: short, with slumped shoulders and a cardigan. Shuffling through the room in his slippers, he always seemed bored and tired and apathetic. You could overhear him, from the dining room, haggling with customers about portion sizes and prices. There were a lot of arguments in that town; people were always convinced they were getting ripped off. I always imagined that, inevitably, one of those arguments would erupt into a gun battle. Anyway, the wife was always separate from that. She was in the back, with a white light glowing all around her, at least in my mind.

We always ordered the same exact things: wonton soup, which my mom called "honton," shrimp with lobster sauce, and roast pork fried rice—all for about four dollars, complete with an egg roll. The wife/chef went back and forth between the dining room and the kitchen, taking orders and cooking them. To me, she was unbelievably glamorous. Looking back, she was the epitome of what a person in a restaurant should be: she was charming, charismatic, and accommodating. She made you feel taken care of and happy, even though it was far from fine dining. She really made a mark on me, because she was from a totally different

culture and yet she exhibited the same welcoming behavior my family did. My father used to drive her crazy with special orders and all kinds of inquiries about freshness; she was a saint just for putting up with that. I have tried to live up to her level of graciousness in my restaurants. A customer can order something completely off the menu, and we always say yes, even if it means we have to send someone to the store to buy marshmallows and make s'mores. So she was an influence on me in terms of running a restaurant. The food was an inspiration to me, too. It was a gateway to the Far East, which became a huge part of my repertoire.

A person does not become American, culturally, simply by setting foot in New York. It is a gradual process that is different for each person. Italian-American cuisine evolved from Old World cooking gradually, as well. In both cases, the labels are subjective and the process takes place most dramatically in the first generation. When my grandmother was holding feasts every Sunday, I ate almost exactly as I would have if I had grown up in Southern Italy (in economically good times, that is). As my mother's lifestyle became more urban, she was unable to grow her own produce and raise livestock. Her pantry came to reflect the conveniences of the supermarket. Gradually, the food we ate changed in taste and texture. As part of the first generation born here, I

think, my siblings and I went through our own immigration. We were raised in such a way that going to school was like stepping into a foreign country. At home, we spoke Italian, ate big chunks of bread with the crusts intact, and hardly left the house. We were used to seeing livestock and harvesting broccoli rabe.

One sign to me that I was different from other kids was the experience of going over to friends' houses after school and not being offered anything to eat or drink by their mothers. They didn't try to feed us! It was totally bizarre to me. It seemed strange and not quite right. Yet I also felt embarrassed when people came to my house and my family fussed over them or ordered them to join the entire family for a rowdy feast. It made most of them very uncomfortable; to little kids, the mere notion of sitting around with a bunch of grown-ups is pretty unappealing. There were exceptions, however, and these were quite significant for me. One was Robert Ruiz and another was my good friend Bhaya, who was Indian and totally unfazed by my mother's urge to stuff him full of ravioli, as I was happy to be encouraged to eat more lamb curry and basmati rice at his cousins' house.

It's fascinating for me to look at the immigrant generation of my family—my mother and father and their siblings—and think back to

my childhood. Everyone has become more American, some with effort and some reluctantly. Some can drive and speak English, some can do neither. I have, so far in my life, also become a lot more American and, at least in most superficial ways, less obviously Italian. I was very ethnic as a little kid, emanating bravado to hide my self-consciousness. I had a heavy accent and I wore a lot of gold jewelry, including a large gold cross. When I got a little older, and more aware of the looks I got, I didn't necessarily want to be marked like that. I guess like most kids, I wanted to blend in and not be "weird."

The Americanizing of immigrants, specifically Italians, does not mean a total loss of "Italian-ness," at least not for a couple of generations, and not necessarily ever. Italian-American culture is really its own thing, the melding of two different worlds, and it is different in every family, depending on where in Italy they originated and where in the States they settled. It is defined in terms of intertwined attitudes and values, and the result is reflected in their food. The cuisine changed with our family because the ingredients changed. My relatives don't talk about the differences as much as I would expect. I figured they arrived here and experienced culture shock at the grocery store, but it seems that they gradually and imperceptibly adapted to certain changes without much apprehension or thrill. As they did in Italy, they experiment with things until they figure out the best, most logical products to use. (See The Italian-American Pantry, page 249.)

When they first arrived, my relatives had one basic thing to worry about, and that was survival. They worked and saved as much as they could. Eventually, they were able to re-create a lot of aspects of their lives in the Old World. That is truly impressive, considering they were in a city and had come from farm country and warmer weather. My uncle Joe was a butcher in Italy, and he's a butcher here. He always had access to good meat with an employee's discount and has always made his own sausages and salami. My grandmother re-created her house in Italy on Long Island, with even more farm attached. Out of the basic geographic differences came a new cuisine. Italian and Italian-American cuisines are distinct things.

I think a lot of people in this country have some heritage that they rebuke or underappreciate. You only have to do that for one generation to risk losing the riches of your family's culture forever. Perhaps some people have to go through the process of pushing away the old to figure out their identities, as I did as a teenager in Queens and in my early years as a chef, when I was interested in every cuisine except my own. But I am glad I came around to realizing how valuable my upbringing was and what I have taken from it while the immigrant generation of my family is still around to cook and enjoy that food with me. I have also introduced my relatives to many ingredients and flavors from different parts of the world and other parts of Italy, and they have welcomed those taste experiences, too. They enjoy caviar and stone crabs on Christmas, and have had my Taylor Bay scallops and uni at Union Pacific. I love this exchange of flavors.

Within my family, I was different. I think all teenagers really struggle to define themselves and develop their identities. It's always hard, but I think it was even harder for my parents to let that process run its course. The culture of adolescence usually bewilders parents to some extent, but I was also an American in an Italian household. During those years, I felt like they could tell I was different and couldn't relate to me in some ways, and didn't want me to express those differences because they didn't know how to react. Those differences were typical ones in first-generation kids; I was more Americanized, more interested in the outside world, in different cultures, and in fitting in. I stopped looking ethnic as I got older, I stopped sounding ethnic, I worked in Manhattan and studied in France. The time

© Matthias Gaggl

when we all saw eye to eye was at the dinner table. Eating dinner with your family is really important; it's where sins are washed away. Especially to Italians, missing family dinner is not an option.

I enrolled in the Culinary Institute of America in 1982, when I was sixteen years old. I don't know how articulated the thought was at the time, but I did have a strong sense that I was having a richer experience than other people because of my background and the role food had always played in my life. I had spent so many hours in the kitchen with the women in my family, and had done so much exploring

in New York, that I had a food education without realizing it. Most important, that experience had trained my palate. Learning how good things can taste was the most important part of my education.

On the other hand, at the CIA, I studied the cuisines and techniques that I thought were valuable and that did not include Italian. In terms of technique, French was it. When my relatives saw me, they always asked whether I was going to open an Italian restaurant or why I wasn't cooking Italian food. A few years after I lived in France, around 1986, Italian restaurants started to get a lot of

53

attention, and regional Italian food was becoming familiar to New Yorkers. There were many, many dishes and styles of cooking that I had never heard of, and that my family had never cooked. It made me realize that Italian food was complicated and much more far-reaching than I thought; I had considered it easy and simple. I think that realization made me avoid Italian food in my own repertoire more purposefully. Suddenly, I was an Italian who was intimidated by Italian cuisine!

I still don't know much about regional cooking. I really admire those chefs and writers who have spent sufficient time traveling and eating in Italy to learn about the many different cuisines. Some of those people are Giulliano Bugialli, Faith Willinger, Mario Batali, Biba Caggiano, Marcella Hazan, and Arthur Schwartz. So far, I have approached Italian cooking more in the style of regular Italians from all regions—my own region, Campagna, is the only region. In

Italy, historically, regional identity has made for extremely specific cuisines based strictly on the food that naturally exists in each area. Because of the variety in terrain and climate, one region may thrive on sheep's milk while its neighbor eats almost only fish. So, although many of these regions are small and near one another, they are like different countries, with different dialects, different flavors. Of course, this is becoming less and less strict as the world becomes smaller and smaller, thanks to technology, but still, these traditions run deep.

My region is really New York—Queens and Long Island, not Campagna. It is based on the Campagna region because my whole family is from there, but the Italian-American food tradition is a cuisine in its own right. So, next time you hear some snotty food expert scoff at it, calling it "inauthentic" or "not really Italian," scoff back that he could be so ignorant. It is not "authentically" Italian; it is a cuisine that originated from the relocation of people and the new existence of a cuisine in a foreign land. That actually describes the development of every cuisine in history. "Authentic" doesn't really mean anything if you take into consideration the fact that Italian cuisine didn't originally include noodles or tomatoes. It seems it's just a matter of time until a cuisine gains the status of standing on its own. Let's start to recognize the Italian-

American cuisine now. It encompasses a full and unique set of ingredients and techniques. It's fascinating to watch it develop in the United States, because, as you will see, although the core of Italian-American cuisine is based on Campagna, Sicily, and Apuglia, there is wider regionality here since people from different regions in Italy moved to different places in America. For example, the Little Italy in San Francisco has a lot of Genovese food.

Although my family's rich life in the kitchen and at the table planted the seed in me that eventually motivated me to go to culinary school and become a chef, I spent my professional life, until a few years ago, focusing on classic techniques in French cooking and applying it to my own voice at Union Pacific. I enjoy creating food based on flavors I love and experimenting with the techniques I know. But then I have this completely different side, the side that wants my mom's frittatas always to taste exactly as I remember them, the side that just wants to celebrate the joy of being around the table with my family.

I had to move in a totally different direction in food in order to come back to my roots. I guess like any kid, it was important to explore the world and define myself outside of family life. And I am glad I did, but I am also extremely happy that I didn't stray for too long and that the older generation of my family is still right on Long Island. As I started to think more and more about my mother's and grandmother's food, I had an urge to share it with the world. I thought, what if a restaurant could provide the feelings of joy that I experience at the table with my relatives? If the food was really prepared as my mother and her sisters-in-law would cook at home, and the guests could relax and enjoy one another's company? And at the same time, this place could be an homage to my grandmother, my mother, my aunts and uncles, and the cuisine created by immigrants.

These were the ideas I was entertaining more and more when I was approached by Mark Burnett and NBC to do a TV show about a restaurant. Their idea was to make a documentary-style reality show about the public place that has more passion and drama than any other: the restaurant. Most Americans have at some point worked in a restaurant, even if it was a summer job at the local hamburger joint when they were fourteen, so they have glimpsed the extreme pressure and adrenaline of the kitchen and the service in a restaurant. It was a great idea.

Because of the schedule of the show and all the planning that went into finding and redesigning the space, hiring and training a staff, and developing the menu, things happened really fast when we opened Rocco's.

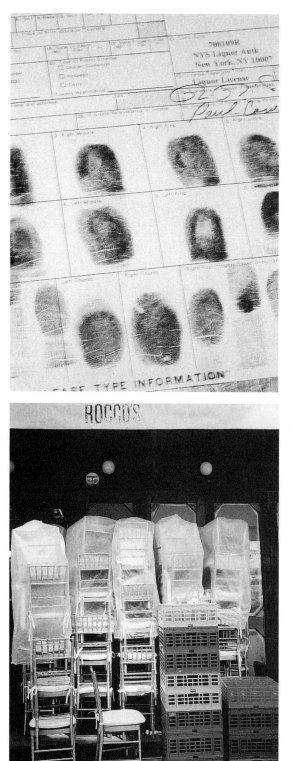

We had just five weeks to do it all! Normally, this process would go on for as many months. Thank God my family was on hand and happy to help me with the food. My mother, aunts, and uncle spent hours talking with me and my kitchen staff about their food, letting us taste things and teaching us how to "make it happen." It was an invaluable education; they are such a treasure to me for their knowledge and passion. The recipes in this book include those that my cooks learned in the kitchen at Rocco's and more.

If the restaurant was my way of sharing the good life with the world, this book goes even further. Once we opened, people from all over the country started calling and asking for my mother's meatball recipe (see page 78), and I realized that I should share everything they have taught me. There is magic at the table when you eat this food, and even more if you cook it in your own home than if you eat it in a restaurant.

I immigrated from an Italian culture to an American culture, and I fought hard to do that. It was my own process, and it was not unlike that of my parents, who fought to become American. The first generation born here has a decision to make about who to be. It's not one or the other, usually; I think it's more often a struggle to find the right balance. When I finally came out of that process, around age thirty, I had

become American, yet my Italian background was readily and happily a part of my life. The combination of experiencing the food culture at home and living in a diverse neighborhood opened my eyes to food and the world. My formal training was the final layer of a rich education in food, but my mom's training was the most important.

Ultimately, I am extremely grateful for having had such rich experiences. Take it from me, you don't have to go missing from your background in order to appreciate it, but if you have turned your back to old traditions, it's not too late to get back to them, or create new ones.

SPECIAL MENUS

Christmas Eve: The Seven Fishes

Clams Oreganata (page 84)

Cold Scungilli Salad (page 87)

Fried Baccalà (page 91)

Spaghettini with Crab Sauce (page 122)

Stewed Baccalà (page 155)

Broiled Octopus (page 153)

Broiled Lobster Tails (page 159)

Biscotti (page 230)

Elena's Ricotta Grain Cake (page 234)

Christmas

Josephine's Stuffed Mushrooms (page 83)

Nicolina's Lasagne (page 127)

Filet Mignon (page 188)

Sfringi (page 231)

Easter

Stuffed Artichokes (page 82)

Cavatelli Marinara (page 134)

Rabbit Cacciatora (page 182)

Baby Lamb Brodedatto (page 175)

Verdure, Room Temperature (page 198)

Zia Elena's Easter Cookies (page 228)

Sunday Supper

Eggplant Rollatini (page 76)

Stuffed Roasted Peppers (page 196)

Rigatoni al Ragù (page 120)

Chopped Salad (page 204)

Zeppole (page 236)

Friday Dinner

Crispy Lemony Shrimp (page 86)

Spaghettini Aglio e Olio (page 123)

Grilled Trout, Porgy, or Sea Bass (page 152)

String Beans Patata (page 199)

Elena's Cream Puffs (page 229)

The Italian-American Diet Dinner

Escarole Soup (page 107)

Chicken with Chunky Lemon Sauce (page 170)

Braised Fennel (page 195)

After-School Treats

Pizza Fritta (page 92)

Mama's Frittata (page 101)

Meatball Heros (page 223)

Elena's Blueberry Cake (page 238)

Good Friday

Calamari Fritta (page 92)

Bucatini with Anchovies (page 126)

Oil and Vinegar Bass in a Pouch (page 157)

Stolen Dandelions (page 199)

Zabaglione (page 236)

I talians usually have antipasto as a shared first course consisting of many little dishes, so this section includes a lot of good ideas for entertaining, lunching, and snacking. At my grandmother's house, a very long table, especially from the perspective of a little kid, was filled with an abundance of choices at the beginning of every feast.

Throughout this book are recipes my mom developed, perfecting them over the years. Many of her great recipes are antipasti, like her meatballs of course, but on the following pages are more of her best-loved creations. I am including a few other favorites from my relatives. They were all, like my mom, inspired by my grandmother's cooking.

Mama's Classic Antipasti

Eggplant Rollatini

As kids, my siblings and I used to flip out whenever my mom made this dish or any other that was rolled up. (See Veal Spiedini, page 77.) I still get pretty excited, actually. It's not the novelty of rolling, it is the way it brings all the flavors and textures together: the smooth creaminess of the ricotta with the crunchy eggplant and tangy, sweet marinara.

ACTIVE TIME ~ 1 hr. TOTAL TIME ~ 1 hr. PORTIONS ~ 6

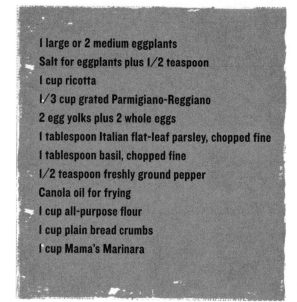

1 large or 2 medium eggplants
Salt for eggplants plus 1/2 teaspoon
1 cup ricotta
1/3 cup grated Parmigiano-Reggiano
2 egg yolks plus 2 whole eggs
1 tablespoon Italian flat-leaf parsley, chopped fine
1 tablespoon basil, chopped fine
1/2 teaspoon freshly ground pepper
Canola oil for frying
1 cup all-purpose flour
1 cup plain bread crumbs
1 cup Mama's Marinara

1. Preheat the oven to 350° F.

2. Cut the top off the eggplants. If your eggplant is very narrow toward the top, trim a few inches so you will get close to even-width slices. Turn the eggplant to stand on its now flat head. Use a very sharp knife to slice it in 12 very thin (1/8-inch) slices, lengthwise. Save a few scraps to use for testing the oil, but discard the outer slices. Spread the slices out on a cookie sheet or on several paper towels and salt them generously, turning them over to salt both sides. Let them sit for about 10 minutes. The salt will draw out a lot of moisture, which you will see as it gathers. It will also make the eggplant a lot more pliable.

3. To make the rollatini filling, put the ricotta, Parmigiano-Reggiano, 2 egg yolks, and the parsley, basil, and pepper in a medium bowl and mix well until the color is uniform. Put the filling in the refrigerator.

4. Fill a deep, heavy stockpot 1/3 of the way up with canola oil and set over high heat. Pat the eggplant slices dry with paper towels and rest them on more paper towels near the stove. Wipe the cookie rack dry. Put the flour, 2 eggs, and bread crumbs in individual shallow, wide bowls. Beat the eggs lightly with a fork. Arrange the bowls near the stove.

5. If you have a thermometer, check the oil to see that it has reached 375° F. If not, test the heat with a scrap of eggplant or flick a little water into the pot (from afar!). It should sizzle vigorously as soon as it hits the oil. Dredge the eggplant in flour, then eggs, then bread crumbs. With each step, be sure to coat both sides of each slice. Then lower them into the oil very carefully. Turn each slice over at least once and remove them with a slotted spoon when they are golden brown, about 2-3 minutes each. Place them back on the cookie rack. Let them cool for about 8-10 minutes.

6. Remove the filling from the fridge. To make the rollatini, scoop a heaping tablespoon of the ricotta mixture onto each piece of eggplant, about an inch from the thicker edge. Then roll that edge over the ricotta and to the top. Place them seam-side down in a 10-inch square casserole or a similar container. They should fit snugly to keep the rollatini from unrolling. Ladle about a cup of marinara over the rollatini. They should not be entirely covered. Bake for about 10 minutes, until they are warm throughout. Serve them hot.

Veal Spiedini

The key is to get the veal as thin as possible, so save up all the annoying things that happened during the day, grab a mallet or a heavy pan, and get pounding. But make sure to put the veal between two sheets of wax paper or plastic wrap, or cleaning the kitchen will be the next annoying thing you have to do. I love to grill the veal over fire, but if you are cooking at home, the broiler works wonderfully.

ACTIVE TIME ~ 25 min. TOTAL TIME ~ 30 min. PORTIONS ~ 4

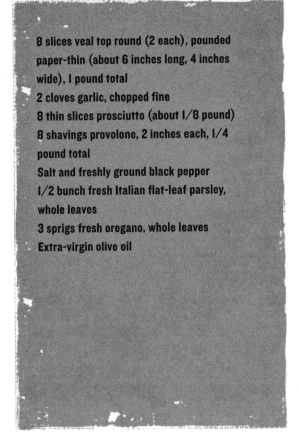

8 slices veal top round (2 each), pounded paper-thin (about 6 inches long, 4 inches wide), 1 pound total

2 cloves garlic, chopped fine

8 thin slices prosciutto (about 1/8 pound)

8 shavings provolone, 2 inches each, 1/4 pound total

Salt and freshly ground black pepper

1/2 bunch fresh Italian flat-leaf parsley, whole leaves

3 sprigs fresh oregano, whole leaves

Extra-virgin olive oil

1. Preheat the broiler.

2. Lay a few sheets of wax paper or plastic wrap on your work surface. Then lay a couple of slices of veal on top, spaced out by a few inches, and place another layer of plastic or wax paper on top. Pound the meat with a flat, sided, heavy mallet or the bottom of a small cast-iron skillet. Make sure the veal is very thin but doesn't tear, and check that all the slices are roughly the same size and thickness so they cook at the same rate. Trim the edges of irregularly shaped ones if necessary. Set them aside.

3. Now, stuff the veal. Work with the slices laid out flat, with the short ends at top and bottom. Because the veal will be rolled up, it is important not to overstuff each slice. First, lay 1 slice of prosciutto on each slice of veal, covering the whole surface. Fold the prosciutto if necessary, or trim it to fit. Add 1 slice of provolone down the center. Then sprinkle each veal slice with a tiny bit of garlic, salt, pepper, parsley, and oregano.

4. Roll the spiedini, from bottom to top, lining up the edges as well as you can. Stick a toothpick all the way through, being sure to pin down the edge. Brush each spiedini with olive oil all around, and place in the broiler on a broiler pan for about 2 minutes on each side, or until golden brown. The cheese should melt and keep the spiedini closed when you pull out the toothpicks.

Mama's Meatballs

My mother is known better for these meatballs than she ever could have imagined. In Italy, meatballs, or *polpette*, are usually a lot smaller and, weird as it may seem, never eaten with pasta. They are served alone or in soup. In the United States, they became a lot bigger and are eaten alone, on heros, with spaghetti, and even on pizza. There are a lot of meatballs out there, folks, and I'm sure you have tasted your fair share, but I believe these are the best meatballs in the world. I can't, to this day, pinpoint what it is that makes them so phenomenal; I think it is largely the fact that she mixes and rolls them by hand. They are not dense like many meatballs, but they also don't fall apart in tomato sauce. It's not just my bias speaking here; everyone loves them. People who hate pork love them; people who never go near veal can't get enough. Vegetarians make exceptions for them. I encourage you to make these meatballs your own. Your kids will love something you make by hand, too.

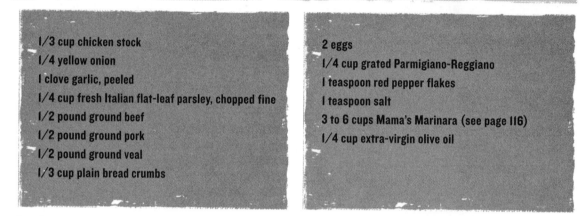

ACTIVE TIME ~ 40 min.   **TOTAL TIME** ~ 1 hr., 30 min.   **PORTIONS** ~ 4 (20 meatballs)

1/3 cup chicken stock	2 eggs
1/4 yellow onion	1/4 cup grated Parmigiano-Reggiano
1 clove garlic, peeled	1 teaspoon red pepper flakes
1/4 cup fresh Italian flat-leaf parsley, chopped fine	1 teaspoon salt
1/2 pound ground beef	3 to 6 cups Mama's Marinara (see page 116)
1/2 pound ground pork	1/4 cup extra-virgin olive oil
1/2 pound ground veal	
1/3 cup plain bread crumbs	

1. Place the chicken stock, garlic, and onions in a blender or food processor and purée.

2. In a large bowl, combine the puréed stock mix, meat, bread crumbs, eggs, Parmigiano-Reggiano, red pepper flakes, and salt. Combine with both hands until the mixture is uniform. Do not overmix.

3. Put a little olive oil on your hands and form the mixture into balls a little larger than golf balls. They should be about 1/4 cup each, though if you prefer bigger or smaller, it will only affect the browning time.

4. Pour about 1/2 inch of extra-virgin olive oil into a straight-sided, 10-inch-wide sauté pan and heat over a medium-high flame. Add the meatballs to the pan (working in batches, if necessary) and brown the meatballs well on all sides. This will take about 10-15 minutes.

5. While the meatballs are browning, heat the marinara sauce in a stockpot over medium heat. Lift the meatballs out of the sauté pan with a slotted spoon and put them in the marinara sauce. Stir gently. Simmer for one hour.

6. Serve with a little extra Parmigiano-Reggiano sprinkled on top.

Uncle Joe's Sausages

My uncle Joe has built military bases in Italy, been a cow-milker in Venezuela, and worked as a landscaper in Long Island. First and foremost, he is a butcher. At Rocco's, he made his famous sausages from scratch with the help of his wife, Elena. For a home cook this just requires a little time and a sausage stuffer. If you don't have one, keep in mind these are great out of the casing. Especially for pasta, the meat mixture can be crumbled and browned loose rather than in individual links. (See Orecchiette with Broccoli Rabe and Sausage, page 137)

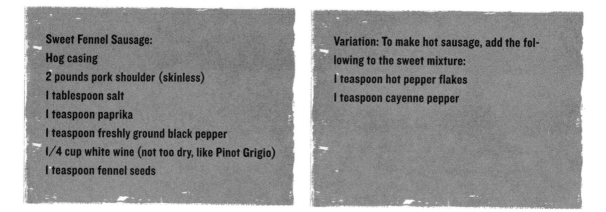

ACTIVE TIME ~ 30 min. TOTAL TIME ~ 30 min. PORTIONS ~ 4 (8 sausages)

Sweet Fennel Sausage:

Hog casing

2 pounds pork shoulder (skinless)

1 tablespoon salt

1 teaspoon paprika

1 teaspoon freshly ground black pepper

1/4 cup white wine (not too dry, like Pinot Grigio)

1 teaspoon fennel seeds

Variation: To make hot sausage, add the following to the sweet mixture:

1 teaspoon hot pepper flakes

1 teaspoon cayenne pepper

1. Use natural hog casing to make links. It comes packed in salt. In order to get rid of the overwhelming salt flavor and to rehydrate the casing so it doesn't rip, rinse the casing very well with cold water, also making sure to rinse the insides as well. Then submerge all the casing in water for at least a few hours or overnight. Remove the casing and drain the excess water.

2. In a large mixing bowl or even on a big wooden work surface, combine the pork and all the other ingredients well with your hands. Using a sausage machine, fill the casing with the sausage mix according to the manufacturer's instructions. Use butcher's twine to make 3- to 4-ounce links. The sausages should be about 4 inches long each.

Uncle Joe's Sausage & Peppers

ACTIVE TIME ~ 20 min.   **TOTAL TIME** ~ 45 min.   **PORTIONS** ~ 4

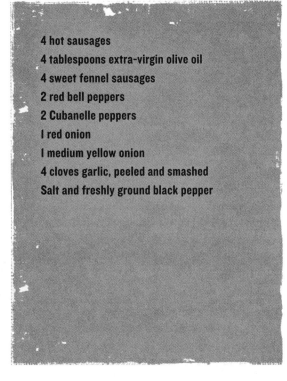

4 hot sausages

4 tablespoons extra-virgin olive oil

4 sweet fennel sausages

2 red bell peppers

2 Cubanelle peppers

I red onion

I medium yellow onion

4 cloves garlic, peeled and smashed

Salt and freshly ground black pepper

1. Sear the sausages in a large skillet with the olive oil over high heat, 5-7 minutes. Make sure to brown them on all sides. They do not have to be cooked through since they will be cooked more later. Remove them from the pan and set aside. Turn off the heat.

2. Meanwhile, cut the red bell and Cubanelle peppers in half lengthwise, remove the stems, seeds, and veins, and cut the peppers into long strips about 1/2 inch thick. Cut the onions in half and then in 1/2-inch-thick slices.

3. In the same sauté pan in which you seared the sausages, sauté the garlic over medium-low heat for 3-4 minutes, or until it is tender and light golden brown. Add the onions and peppers and cook slowly, stirring occasionally, for 10 minutes. They will become soft and very sweet, and they will let out some of their moisture and shrink in size. Add the sausages, and sauté until they are cooked through, about 15 minutes.

4. Season the mixture with salt and pepper to taste. Cut the sausages in half on a slant, into thick slices, or leave them whole to serve. You can also eat them in hot-dog buns, the way they are served at street fairs.

Stuffed Artichokes

Artichokes are always reserved for special occasions in my family. We usually eat them stuffed on Easter. This is one of my mother's specialties. At the restaurant, we added a slice of pancetta, chopped, to the filling, which is a great variation. This is a great dish to serve when friends come over, because they will have to use their hands, which usually makes any party more fun and casual.

ACTIVE TIME ~ 20 min. TOTAL TIME ~ 1 hr., 15 min. PORTIONS ~ 4

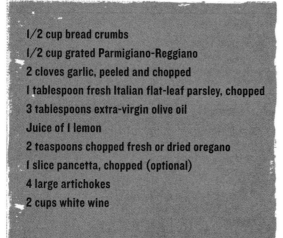

1/2 cup bread crumbs

1/2 cup grated Parmigiano-Reggiano

2 cloves garlic, peeled and chopped

1 tablespoon fresh Italian flat-leaf parsley, chopped

3 tablespoons extra-virgin olive oil

Juice of 1 lemon

2 teaspoons chopped fresh or dried oregano

1 slice pancetta, chopped (optional)

4 large artichokes

2 cups white wine

1. For the filling: combine the bread crumbs, Parmigiano-Reggiano, garlic, parsley, olive oil, lemon juice, and oregano in a medium bowl. Add the pancetta now if you choose to use it.

2. Trim the stems off the artichokes and pull off the tough outer leaves. Make sure the bottoms are flat so the artichokes can stand up. With your fingers, spread the leaves apart as much as you can while you stuff the bread crumb mixture between them. Put plenty of the filling on top.

3. Put the artichokes in a sauce pot with high enough sides that you can stand the artichokes up. Pour the wine into the pot. Place the pot over medium heat and gently simmer for 30-45 minutes covered. They will be done when you can easily pull the leaves off and the meaty bit on each one is tender. The artichokes will darken as they steam.

Josephine's Stuffed Mushrooms

My youngest cousin, Josephine, re-created stuffed mushrooms, a dish my mother and her mother, Elena, made on special occasions. Josephine's version has cheddar cheese, which, of course, is not an Italian ingredient. But among other things, she inherited a palate that allowed her to try it, and it works. The sharpness of the cheddar is a great complement to the mushroom. Who knew? If you're too scared, substitute provolone. Josephine's other secret is her electric stovetop. I think this is the first time I've wished I had one. To melt the cheese into the filling, she turns the heat off completely, using the residual heat of the electric burner which takes a few minutes to cool down. To mimic that effect, I suggest turning the stove down to almost nothing when you add the cheese, and then turning it off completely. If you have an electric stove, this is your time to shine.

ACTIVE TIME ~ 5 min. TOTAL TIME ~ 45 min. PORTIONS ~ 4

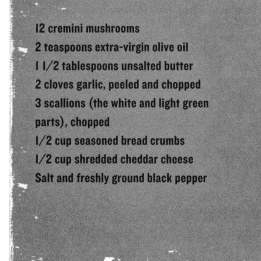

12 cremini mushrooms

2 teaspoons extra-virgin olive oil

1 1/2 tablespoons unsalted butter

2 cloves garlic, peeled and chopped

3 scallions (the white and light green parts), chopped

1/2 cup seasoned bread crumbs

1/2 cup shredded cheddar cheese

Salt and freshly ground black pepper

1. Preheat the oven to 350° F.

2. Remove the stems from the mushrooms and trim just the bottom ends. Chop the stems and set aside. Place the caps round side down in a baking dish greased with the olive oil.

3. Melt the butter in a large skillet over medium heat. Add the garlic, scallions, and mushroom stems, and cook until tender, about 5 minutes. Add the bread crumbs and stir to combine all the ingredients into the consistency of paste. Turn the heat down as low as possible and add the cheese to the mixture. Mix the cheese until it is melted and combined with all the other ingredients. Remove the skillet from the heat immediately. Stuff the mushroom caps with the mixture. Bake the mushrooms for 30 minutes. If the tops are not golden brown, put them back in for about 5 minutes more.

Clams Oreganata

This is an Italian-American restaurant favorite. Be sure to preheat your broiler as soon as you begin, because the key to golden, crunchy bread crumbs is high heat. If you can find fresh oregano for this dish, it makes a big difference, but of course dried is fine, too.

ACTIVE TIME ~ 5 min.   TOTAL TIME ~ 20 min.   PORTIONS ~ 4

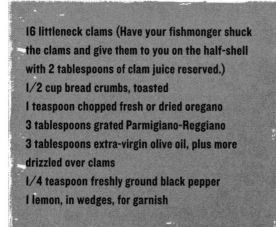

16 littleneck clams (Have your fishmonger shuck the clams and give them to you on the half-shell with 2 tablespoons of clam juice reserved.)

1/2 cup bread crumbs, toasted

1 teaspoon chopped fresh or dried oregano

3 tablespoons grated Parmigiano-Reggiano

3 tablespoons extra-virgin olive oil, plus more drizzled over clams

1/4 teaspoon freshly ground black pepper

1 lemon, in wedges, for garnish

1. Preheat the broiler.

2. In a medium bowl, mix together the bread crumbs, oregano, Parmigiano-Reggiano, reserved 2 tablespoons clam juice, olive oil, and black pepper to taste. Top the clams with this mixture generously, but don't pack the bread crumbs down. Drizzle with a little olive oil.

3. Place them in the broiler until the clams are tender and just cooked through and the bread-crumb mix is crispy and golden brown, 7-8 minutes. Serve with lemon wedges.

Crispy Lemony Shrimp

My mother invented this dish years ago using flawless logic. How could you go wrong with shrimp, lemon, garlic, and golden, crunchy bread crumbs? This makes a great appetizer, and because it's good at room temperature, it works wonderfully at a cocktail party.

ACTIVE TIME ~ 15 min. TOTAL TIME ~ 35 min. PORTIONS ~ 4

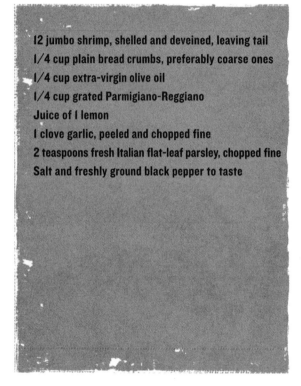

12 jumbo shrimp, shelled and deveined, leaving tail

1/4 cup plain bread crumbs, preferably coarse ones

1/4 cup extra-virgin olive oil

1/4 cup grated Parmigiano-Reggiano

Juice of 1 lemon

1 clove garlic, peeled and chopped fine

2 teaspoons fresh Italian flat-leaf parsley, chopped fine

Salt and freshly ground black pepper to taste

1. Preheat the oven to 350° F. Rinse the shrimp and dry them well with paper towels.

2. Toss the bread crumbs with the olive oil and the Parmigiano-Reggiano. Toast the mixture on a baking sheet until golden brown and crunchy, about 8 minutes. Set aside to cool for a few minutes. Raise the oven heat to 450° F. You will use your baking sheet again.

3. In a large, wide bowl, toss the shrimp with the lemon juice, garlic, parsley, and a pinch each of salt and pepper. When the bread crumbs have cooled off, add them to the same bowl and toss them together with the shrimp.

4. Lay the shrimp on the baking sheet or in a large cast-iron skillet. They should be coated with the bread-crumb mixture. There may be excess breading. Sprinkle about 1 tablespoon over the shrimp and discard the rest. Be sure to spread the shrimp out in one layer so they get evenly crispy.

5. Bake the shrimp until they are cooked through but not hard, about 10 minutes. Season to taste with salt, and serve.

Cold Scungilli Salad

Christmas Eve would not be Christmas Eve without this dish. The version below is my mother's. I love it, but you can play around with the elements as you like without much of a threat of messing it up. My aunt Elena makes a very simple version, using just shrimp, calamari, scungilli, lemon, olive oil, and lots of celery. Try to chop all the vegetables roughly the same size, about 1/2-inch chunks.

ACTIVE TIME ~ 15 min. TOTAL TIME ~ overnight plus 1 hr., 15 min. PORTIONS ~ 4

1/4 cup extra-virgin olive oil

2 tablespoons white wine vinegar

Juice of 3 lemons

Pinch of salt

Pinch of freshly ground black pepper

1/4 pound calamari, in rings

1/4 pound shrimp, shelled, deveined, and chopped

1/4 pound scungilli, sliced thin (This is conch—often sold frozen; if so, buy 1/3 pound since it will thaw and decrease weight.)

3 stalks celery, rinsed and chopped

2 plum tomatoes, chopped

4 cremini mushroom caps, chopped

1 red bell pepper, stem and seeds removed, chopped

1 cucumber, cored and chopped

1/2 bunch fresh Italian flat-leaf parsley, chopped

Large pinch of red pepper flakes

1. Bring a big pot of water to a boil. Pour the olive oil and vinegar in a small bowl; squeeze the lemons over that bowl and add the salt and pepper. Mix together with a fork. That's your dressing.

2. Combine all the other ingredients aside from the seafood in a plastic container, if you have one that's large enough, or in a large Ziploc bag. Pour the dressing in and mix everything together.

3. Prepare an ice bath. Blanch all the seafood just until the shrimp gains its orange color. Quickly drain and put the fish into an ice bath for about 1 minute. Drain the cold water, shake off excess, and combine with the rest of the salad in the plastic container.

4. Refrigerate the container overnight. Remove the container at least 1 hour before serving, so it will achieve room temperature before serving.

5. The fish should have a tender consistency, not chewy, and it will pick up a lot of flavor from the other ingredients.

Fried foods are some of southern Italy's best moves. The region has really perfected the quick-fried, fresh technique. I think Americans see fried food as heavy and decadent, but when you're working with delicate, ethereal tastes, like fish, shrimp, and zucchini, frying quickly at a high temperature is one of the best ways to capture the flavor. The "friedness" and the salt should be background elements. The key to that perfect, light crispiness is to start by making sure whatever you are frying is completely dry, then give it a very thin dusting of flour just before frying.

The ideal temperature differs depending on the food. Most of the recipes that follow require that the oil be heated to at least 350° F. Otherwise, whatever is being fried will absorb the oil, and the result will be soggy and lacking most of its original taste. I recommend buying a candy thermometer to test the temperature of the oil. If you are working without one, test the oil by frying one small piece of whatever you are working with. It should seize up and brown quickly. If you put a piece of zucchini in your oil and it just floats there, not sizzling and spitting, the oil is not nearly hot enough. It should be almost smoking. You can also test by wetting your fingers and sprinkling the oil (from afar!). If it does not sizzle on contact, raise the heat and wait a few minutes.

Also, be sure not to crowd the pot. Fry in batches if there isn't room for everything to brown at once. If you put too much in the oil at a time, it will bring the temperature down, and because pieces are touching one another, they will not be exposed to enough oil for the surfaces to crisp. Be very careful when you put the food in the oil. Don't drop things from high above the pot, and always wear long sleeves. Use the biggest, heaviest stockpot you have, and fill it no more than halfway with oil.

Let the following pages inspire you to fry different vegetables; I especially love cauliflower, eggplant slices, and, of course, potato. And if you buy a mandoline, you'll be looking for projects.

Fritti

Fried Baccalà

Unless my brother was involved, you could never find fish sticks in my house. This was the closest we got. We always eat fried baccalà on Christmas Eve. This is my aunt Maria's recipe.

ACTIVE TIME ~ 15 min.   TOTAL TIME ~ 4 days, 15 min.   PORTIONS ~ 4

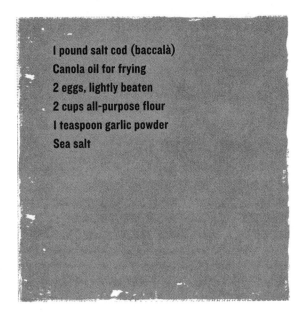

I pound salt cod (baccalà)
Canola oil for frying
2 eggs, lightly beaten
2 cups all-purpose flour
I teaspoon garlic powder
Sea salt

1. Submerge the salt cod in cold water in a large container and soak in the refrigerator for 4 days, changing the water once or twice each day. Drain and dry the fish by wrapping it in paper towels before frying.

2. While the fish is drying, heat a large pot filled 1/3 up with canola oil. Put the eggs in a wide, shallow bowl and the flour, with garlic powder mixed in, in another bowl.

3. With a sharp knife, cut the fish into 1-inch chunks. The shape does not matter. Dredge each piece in flour, then in the egg wash, then the flour again. Make sure to coat all sides. Fry the fish in the oil until it is golden brown all around, about 2-3 minutes. Remove the fish from the oil and sprinkle it with sea salt to taste. Let stand on a rack to drain any excess oil, about 1 minute. Serve immediately.

Pizza Fritta

Fried pizza dough: how could that not be delicious? This is the first thing I remember ever making with my mother. It is pan-fried, not deep-fried, and the dough puffs up right before your eyes. My mom used the same small cast-iron pan every time. To me, she was a genius; using leftover bits of regular bread dough, she made this puffy, crispy, sweet stuff. I could not fathom how she got two entirely different things out of one very simple dough. It really is versatile. It can even be savory, topped with Parmigiano-Reggiano cheese and red pepper flakes. My mom used to make fun shapes like dogs or people with the scraps of dough, as her mother had when she was young.

ACTIVE TIME ~ 20 min.   TOTAL TIME ~ 2 hr., 20 min.   PORTIONS ~ 4

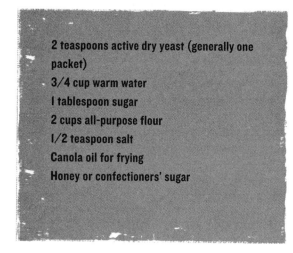

2 teaspoons active dry yeast (generally one packet)

3/4 cup warm water

I tablespoon sugar

2 cups all-purpose flour

I/2 teaspoon salt

Canola oil for frying

Honey or confectioners' sugar

1. Put the yeast in a liquid measuring cup with the water. Stir in the sugar briefly with a fork. If bubbles do not begin to rise within a few minutes, your yeast is not active. Start over with a fresh pack.

2. Put the flour and salt in a deep bowl. The yeast and water mixture should double in volume and be topped with foam after about 10 minutes. At that point, pour it into the bowl with the flour and knead it with your hands until it comes together. Take it out of the bowl and knead it for about 5 minutes on a work surface. When it is smooth and somewhat elastic, roll the dough into a ball, return it to the deep bowl, and cover it with a heavy kitchen towel. Place the bowl in a warm place for 2 hours or until it has about doubled.

3. Push down the dough and place it on a work surface. Gently push it down into a flat, 1/2-inch-thick slab. You can cut it into small pieces or leave it whole and cut it after frying it. Shape it as you wish. Heat canola oil over high heat in a small cast-iron skillet. It should be about 1/2 inch deep. Carefully place the pizza fritta in the skillet. It should sizzle and puff up. Turn it over once, so both sides are light golden brown. It should take about 5 minutes altogether. Place it on a paper towel briefly to blot the excess oil. Serve with honey or confectioners' sugar.

Calamari Fritti

For my family, this is a restaurant treat more than home cooking. Every Italian-American restaurant has fried calamari, most use way too much breading, which either becomes soggy or forms a thick, hard shell around the squid, which steams inside and gets tough and chewy. In the recipe below, the calamari is tender with a thin, crisp outside, not outshined by the breading. In fact, there is no breading per se, just a little flour. Always buy whole squid, and never throw out the tentacles! Use clean oil for frying squid, especially because it will really pick up the flavor of used oil, and that's a damn shame.

ACTIVE TIME ~ 10 min. TOTAL TIME ~ 25 min. PORTIONS ~ 4

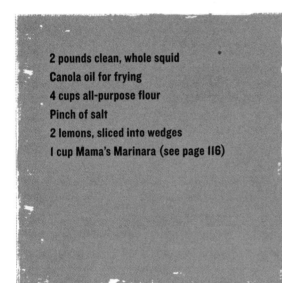

2 pounds clean, whole squid

Canola oil for frying

4 cups all-purpose flour

Pinch of salt

2 lemons, sliced into wedges

1 cup Mama's Marinara (see page 116)

1. Pull the tentacles off the calamari, leaving them in bunches. Slice the calamari into thin rings. Spread the squid out on paper towels and pat dry.

2. Make sure the squid is completely dry before frying. Heat enough canola oil to fill a deep, heavy pot 1/3 up. If you have a thermometer, test that the oil has reached 375°F. If not, do one test calamari ring first. Toss rings and heads a few at a time in the flour, shaking them in a strainer to remove all but a very light coating.

3. When the oil is hot enough, carefully drop the squid in the oil and fry until golden brown. Remove the calamari and place them on a rack. Season them immediately with a generous pinch of salt. Continue frying all the squid in batches, allowing them to cool for about 5 minutes before transferring them to a serving plate. Serve with lemon wedges and warm marinara.

Zucchini Chips

Invest in a mandoline. You will notice that it starts to come in handy all the time for salads and fried things especially. Otherwise, sharpen your knife and slice the zucchini in rounds as paper-thin as possible. They should be translucent. I have tested everything, and although in this country matchsticks are more common, the typical Neapolitan "chip" shape makes crispier zucchini. Make sure to salt the sliced zucchini to remove excess water before frying.

ACTIVE TIME ~ 15 min. TOTAL TIME ~ 25 min. PORTIONS ~ 4

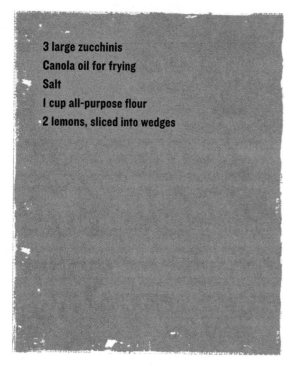

3 large zucchinis
Canola oil for frying
Salt
I cup all-purpose flour
2 lemons, sliced into wedges

1. Using a mandoline or sharpened knife, slice the zucchinis into very thin rounds. Toss the rounds with 2 tablespoons of salt in a colander and shake to coat all the zucchini.

2. Spread the salted zucchini on paper towels to draw out the excess moisture. This will make for a crunchy zucchini chip. Skipping this step will mean soggy fried zucchini, because it has so much water in it that the dusting of flour on the outside would otherwise be wet immediately. Heat the canola oil in a deep, heavy-bottomed stockpot. It should be around 350° F for frying. Toss the zucchini with the flour in a dry strainer or colander to shake off any excess flour.

3. Carefully drop the zucchini chips into the hot oil and fry them until they are golden brown, about 1–2 minutes. Fry only a handful at a time so the temperature of the oil does not drop drastically. Spread out the chips on a cooling rack to drain any excess oil. Taste and season with sea salt, if needed. Serve immediately with lemon wedges.

Arancini di Telefono

This dish was named for its good looks. *Arancini* means "little oranges" and refers to the appearance, not the taste, of these risotto balls. They get their sunny hue from the saffron-infused broth the risotto cooks in. *Telefono* refers to the curled string of melted mozzarella cheese that will stretch between your mouth and the *arancini*, if it's done right. The oil should be a little less hot than for other fried foods, because the balls are thick and dense and the goal is to heat them throughout without burning the outside.

ACTIVE TIME ~ 35 min.   TOTAL TIME ~ 1 hr., 20 min.   PORTIONS ~ 4 (12 balls)

2 tablespoons extra-virgin olive oil

1/2 yellow onion, peeled and chopped fine

2 small cloves garlic, peeled and chopped fine

1/2 cup arborio rice

1 tablespoon white wine

Salt and freshly ground black pepper

6 cups saffron stock (chicken stock simmered with 1/4 teaspoon saffron until bright yellow)

1/2 cup grated Parmigiano-Reggiano

1/2 pound fresh mozzarella, cut in 1/4-inch cubes

Canola oil for frying

About 1 cup all-purpose flour for dredging

2 eggs, lightly beaten

About 1 cup plain bread crumbs for dredging

1. Heat the olive oil in a stockpot over low heat and add the onion and garlic. Cook about 10 minutes, until translucent. Meanwhile, bring the stock to a boil, then turn off the flame under it. Add the risotto to the onion and garlic and stir for 2-3 minutes to coat in the oil. Raise to medium heat. Add the wine and let it mostly evaporate. Begin ladling in the stock, about 1/2 cup at a time, stirring constantly, waiting for the rice to absorb the stock before adding more. Repeat until the rice is cooked al dente. This should take about 20 minutes altogether. Add the Parmigiano-Reggiano, combine, then transfer the rice to a baking sheet lined with wax paper to cool in the refrigerator.

2. When the risotto has cooled completely, scoop it from the baking sheet and, with your hands, form balls slightly larger than golf balls. Press and roll them between your palms to make them compact. Then push one cube of mozzarella into the center of each ball; cover up the hole you made and smooth it. The balls can be frozen at this stage, if desired; warm them to room temperature before frying.

3. Heat enough canola oil to fill a large stockpot 1/3 up. It should only be hot enough that if you flick a few drops of water in, there is a delay before they pop and sizzle.

4. Dredge the risotto balls in the flour, then in the egg, then in the bread crumbs.

5. Fry the *arancini* till golden brown, about 7-8 minutes, and serve hot.

Fried Baby Artichokes

Baby artichokes are becoming very popular in the United States, which means they are easier to find, especially in the spring. They are generally more tender and they lack the sharp inner leaves and hairy choke of their grown-up counterparts. This means they can be eaten whole, stems and all. They are fried in regular (not extra-virgin) olive oil; they will be fried slowly, picking up a lot of the flavor of the oil and cooking through so the heart is tender.

ACTIVE TIME ~ 20 min. TOTAL TIME ~ 30 min. PORTIONS ~ 4

Olive oil

8 baby artichokes

I cup all-purpose flour

Salt

1. Heat enough oil to fill about 1/2 inch in a medium skillet.

2. Remove the tougher, dark green outside layers of the artichoke. Cut the top 2 inches off the leaves, so the artichoke is flat on top. Trim the end of the stem, about 1/4 inch from the end, leaving the stems attached to the artichokes.

3. Lay the trimmed artichokes on a cutting board or wood counter on their sides. With a wide-bladed, heavy knife, smash the artichokes by placing the blade of a knife flat across the thickest part of the artichoke (the heart) and press down with the heel of your palm. It should not be difficult to flatten the artichokes. You will hear a crunch. Dust them very lightly with flour and carefully (one by one from a short height above) place them in the oil. Fry the artichokes for about 10-15 minutes, turning them to fry on all sides. Adjust the heat to maintain a constant but not vigorous sizzle around the artichokes, turning them over periodically, until they are very crispy. Remove them to a rack to drain the excess oil. Salt them generously and serve.

Fried Shrimp

If you prefer small shrimp, don't worry about deveining them. I like to use large shrimp for frying, though. Leave the shell on for a really crunchy snap.

ACTIVE TIME ~ 10 min. TOTAL TIME ~ 15 min. PORTIONS ~ 4

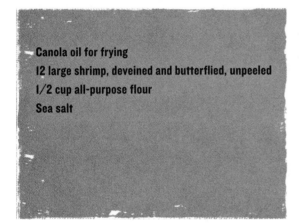

Canola oil for frying

12 large shrimp, deveined and butterflied, unpeeled

1/2 cup all-purpose flour

Sea salt

1. Heat enough canola oil to fill a deep pot 1/3 up. If you have a thermometer, test that the oil has reached 375° F. If not, do one test shrimp first.

2. Make sure the shrimp are completely dry. In a colander, shake the shrimp with a few sprinkles of flour until only a very thin dusting clings to them. Drop them into the hot oil. Do not crowd the pot. Fry for about 5 minutes, until the shrimp are light golden brown. Place them on a rack or a plate covered with paper towels to drain the excess oil, and sprinkle with a few pinches of salt. Serve immediately.

In my house, as in the homes of immigrants and peasants worldwide, eggs are certainly not just for breakfast. They often take the place of meat for dinner. When I was young, the eggs came from my grandmother's hens and had deep orange yolks. In Italy, meat was scarce and eggs had the simple financial advantage that one did not have to slaughter an animal to eat. If you don't happen to have a chicken coop on your property, buy organic whenever possible. Eggs are an excellent, economical source of protein with infinite variations. Almost.

Eggs

Eggs in Purgatory

This is an ingenious dish: eggs poached in slightly spicy tomato sauce. The eggs are poached, in a sense suspended. Perhaps that is the origin of the name. This is a great example of using eggs in the place of meat, a southern Italian practice which proves that eggs don't just come with hash browns and bacon. It's great for dinner, or for a hangover.

ACTIVE TIME ~ 15 min. TOTAL TIME ~ 1 hr. PORTIONS ~ 4

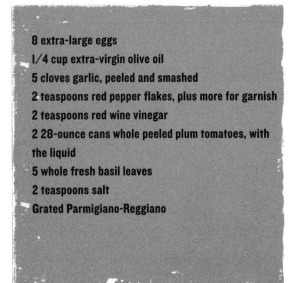

8 extra-large eggs

1/4 cup extra-virgin olive oil

5 cloves garlic, peeled and smashed

2 teaspoons red pepper flakes, plus more for garnish

2 teaspoons red wine vinegar

2 28-ounce cans whole peeled plum tomatoes, with the liquid

5 whole fresh basil leaves

2 teaspoons salt

Grated Parmigiano-Reggiano

1. If your eggs are in the refrigerator, take them out so they can come to room temperature.

2. Preheat oven to 425° F.

3. Make a chunky tomato sauce: heat the olive oil in a large skillet over medium heat. Add the smashed garlic. Stir and further crush the garlic with the edge of a spoon until it is very light brown and tender and has broken down significantly. Add the red pepper flakes and the vinegar.

4. Add the tomatoes, 2 of the basil leaves, and the salt to the pan. Bring it up to a boil, then lower the heat and simmer for 45 minutes to an hour, stirring occasionally to make sure the bottom is not sticking. The tomatoes should break down. You may help them along by pushing down on them with the edge of a spoon. Lower the heat if the sauce begins boiling.

5. Pour the sauce into a casserole with enough surface area for the eggs to sit. Smooth out the top and crack the eggs on top. Bake the casserole in the oven for about 10 minutes, or until the whites cook and the yolks are still runny.

6. Remove the skillet and top with the grated Parmigiano-Reggiano, red pepper flakes to taste, and the other 3 basil leaves, torn by hand. Spoon out the eggs, being careful not to break the yolks, and serve them with toast.

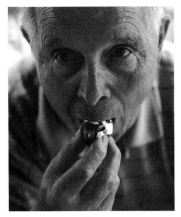

Figs

Eggs

Tomatoes

Box Grater

Hot Pickled Peppers

Broccoli Rabe

Cappicola

Italian Flat Leaf Parsley

Canned Tomato Puree

Anchovies in Olive Oil

Spring Onion

Tripe

Mascarpone

Walnuts

Mozzarella

Home-Canned Tomatoes

Lemons

Bread

Escarole

Garlic

Ricotta

Butcher's Tools

Olives

Artichokes

Fine Cornmeal

Red wine

Ditalini

Onions

Baby Lamb

Dry Pasta

Eggplant

Meat Grinder

Red and Green Bell Pepers and Cubanelles

Parmigiano-Reggiano

Provolone

Red Pepper Flakes

Oregano

Rabbit

Fennel Seeds

Pots and Pans

Mortadella

Rosemary

Fennel

Dried Chick Peas

Extra Virgin Olive Oil

Red Wine Vinegar

Soppressata

Basil

Prosciutto

Salad Greens

Canned Whole Plum Tomotoes

Hazelnuts

Pastina

Ground Beef

Caprese, p. 207

Mama's Frittata

My mom usually brought a frittata to Rosary Society meetings, which I attended just for the food. Everyone brought something, and her frittata was always highly anticipated. But before we could eat, we would stand and say the entire rosary—the whole thing! That took about an hour, and it was worth it, even to a restless kid. The frittata is the Italian omelet, but they are very different. An omelet is a filled egg crepe; a frittata is an egg cake with the garnish incorporated into it evenly. A frittata is more dense, rich, firm, and hearty; it is always browned on both sides and never runny in the center. This is usually eaten in the middle of the day rather than the morning, but if you make one, you'll eat the leftovers at all times. It's the perfect snack.

ACTIVE TIME ~ 15 min. TOTAL TIME ~ 30 min. PORTIONS ~ 12

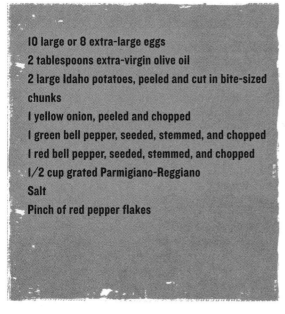

10 large or 8 extra-large eggs
2 tablespoons extra-virgin olive oil
2 large Idaho potatoes, peeled and cut in bite-sized chunks
1 yellow onion, peeled and chopped
1 green bell pepper, seeded, stemmed, and chopped
1 red bell pepper, seeded, stemmed, and chopped
1/2 cup grated Parmigiano-Reggiano
Salt
Pinch of red pepper flakes

1. If your eggs are in the refrigerator, take them out so they can come to room temperature.

2. Heat the olive oil in a 10-inch nonstick pan over medium heat, and sauté the vegetables, stirring often, until tender, about 10–15 minutes. The potatoes should turn a light golden color. Season with salt and pepper.

3. In a bowl, whisk together the eggs and Parmigiano-Reggiano. Season with a pinch of salt and red pepper flakes.

4. Pour the eggs over the softened vegetables and stir gently until the eggs set around the edge of the pan. Stop stirring and continue to cook until the bottom is browned and set, about 6–7 minutes. Flip the frittata and finish cooking on the other side.

5. Slip the frittata out of the pan and slice it into wedges. Serve warm or at room temperature.

Eggs in Polenta

Here's a great example of Italian logic: we feed chickens cornmeal, so why not eat eggs with cornmeal? Whether that's how your mind works or not, runny eggs in creamy, slightly cheesy polenta is unlike anything else. It is a dish that could only have been invented by poor people, who often ate plain polenta for dinner. But the moment when you break the yolk with your fork (or, perhaps more appropriately, your spoon) and stir it into the polenta, well, it doesn't taste like the food of poor farmers.

ACTIVE TIME ~ 15 min.   TOTAL TIME ~ 40 min.   PORTIONS ~ 4

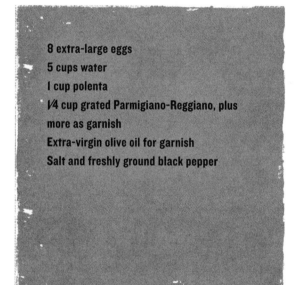

8 extra-large eggs

5 cups water

1 cup polenta

1/4 cup grated Parmigiano-Reggiano, plus more as garnish

Extra-virgin olive oil for garnish

Salt and freshly ground black pepper

1. If your eggs are in the refrigerator, take them out so they can come to room temperature.

2. Preheat the oven to 425° F.

3. Bring the water up to a simmer in a small sauce pot. Slowly pour in the polenta, whisking constantly for 10 minutes. You should have a thick, smooth consistency. Taste to see that there is no bite in the cornmeal. Season with salt and pepper to taste.

4. Remove the pot from the heat and stir in the Parmigiano-Reggiano. Pour the polenta into a casserole and smooth over the top with a spatula. Crack the eggs onto the surface of the polenta.

5. Place the casserole in the oven and bake for 10-15 minutes for firm whites and runny yolks. Drizzle with olive oil, sprinkle with salt, pepper, and more Parmigiano-Reggiano to taste, and serve.

Soup is, hands down, the most comforting, restorative food a person can eat, as far as I am concerned. If chicken noodle soup is Jewish penicillin, pastina is Italian Valium and Prozac all rolled into one. In my home, it was prescribed to anyone feeling under the weather, physically or emotionally. If a bully at school was picking on you, you had the flu or too much homework, soup was the antidote to pouting. And it was easy for my mother and aunts to whip up a bowl for one person at a time, making it a staple snack option for us kids. Part of that was the versatility of soup. Usually, the ingredients were simply pulled out of the pantry. It always started with canned chicken broth. Sometimes there was escarole, sometimes there was an egg dropped in, pastina, potatoes, Parmigiano-Reggiano cheese, chunks of chicken, a piece of bread at the bottom of the bowl, and on and on. In addition to the warmth of the soup, there was something about having my own customized bowl of soup that always made me feel better. The following pages have a few of my favorite versions, but keep soup in mind as a quick, inexpensive cheerer-upper that you can't mess up.

Soup

Pastina

Pastina means "tiny pastas." They are shaped like stars. You should be able to find it in a regular grocery store, or simply use the smallest pasta you can find. This can be embellished upon, as it is practically a clean slate. But sometimes the plainness of something is all you want.

ACTIVE TIME ~ 5 min. TOTAL TIME ~ 15 min. PORTIONS ~ 1

2 cups chicken stock

1 cup pastina

About 1/4 cup grated Parmigiano-Reggiano

Salt and freshly ground black pepper

Chopped parsley to garnish

1. Bring the chicken stock to a boil in a medium sauce pot. Pour in pastina and stir. Cook for about 3-4 minutes, tasting for doneness. They should be slightly firm, since they will continue to cook in the soup. Ladle the soup into bowls and top with Parmigiano-Reggiano, salt, and pepper to taste, and parsley.

Pappa al Pomodoro

Make a habit of checking the house for any one- or two-day-old bread, and make sure to save it from a wrongful death in the garbage can. Of the many reasons never to throw bread away, this soup is number one on my list. Especially when you're on a budget, this soup makes something magnificently satisfying out of nothing. Eat it in late summer when you have overripe tomatoes, or in the winter with canned ones. The cooked bread attains a silky, almost creamy consistency. Be sure to prepare your favorite nap spot in advance.

ACTIVE TIME ~ 10 min. TOTAL TIME ~ 45 min. PORTIONS ~ 4

1 yellow onion, peeled and sliced thin

1 clove garlic, peeled and crushed

1/4 cup extra-virgin olive oil, plus extra-virgin olive oil for garnish

One 8-ounce can whole peeled plum tomatoes, or 3/4 pound peeled, sliced overripe plum tomatoes

1 tablespoon tomato paste

Several slices of day-old Italian or French bread, crumbled

Chicken broth, if necessary

Salt and freshly ground black pepper

Chopped fresh basil for garnish

1. Sauté the onion and garlic in 1/4 cup olive oil until lightly brown. Add the tomatoes and tomato paste (if you are using canned tomatoes, include the liquid in the can). Simmer about 15 minutes, or until the tomatoes have fallen apart. Stir in the bread and a little bit of broth, if necessary, to thin out the mixture. Season with salt and pepper to taste. Stir the mixture over a low flame until it thickens, about 8 minutes. Turn off the heat, cover, and let sit for 15 minutes. Serve sprinkled with freshly chopped basil and extra-virgin olive oil.

Escarole Soup

This is an incredibly easy, tasty, and nourishing soup. Never throw out the rind of Parmigiano-Reggiano. If you have one around, toss it into the broth and let it simmer. This is a very old tradition, and like so many great techniques, it comes from the peasant mentality never to waste any sustenance, especially something with as much flavor as this. As a variation, you can poach marble-size meatballs in the broth (see Mama's Meatballs, page 78).

ACTIVE TIME ~ 5 min. TOTAL TIME ~ 20 min. PORTIONS ~ 4

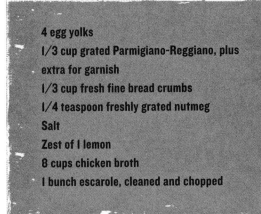

4 egg yolks

1/3 cup grated Parmigiano-Reggiano, plus extra for garnish

1/3 cup fresh fine bread crumbs

1/4 teaspoon freshly grated nutmeg

Salt

Zest of 1 lemon

8 cups chicken broth

1 bunch escarole, cleaned and chopped

1. Mix together egg yolks, Parmigiano-Reggiano, bread crumbs, nutmeg, salt, and lemon zest until firm. Place the broth in a large saucepan and bring it to a simmer. Stir in the escarole and the bread crumb mixture and break it up in the broth. Simmer about 3 minutes. Serve immediately with freshly grated Parmigiano-Reggiano.

Fish Soup

When you buy a whole chicken, you throw the bones into boiling water with some carrots, onions, and herbs to make stock, I hope. Well, this is the fish version, and it makes a really tasty broth that can be used in many ways. In the old days, fish was always bought whole. The heads were never discarded, because they had lots of flavor, as do the bones. Next time you buy a whole fish, ask the fishmonger for the bones (ask for the fish "filleted with bones"). They're usually free. My relatives used to leave the heads right in the soup and eat the fish cheeks and eyeballs. For your crowd, though, you might want to strain it. This is also a great stock to use in making seafood risotto, but if it tastes salty, dilute it with water.

ACTIVE TIME ~ 10 min. TOTAL TIME ~ 4 days, 50 min. PORTIONS ~ 4

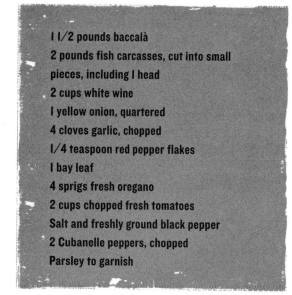

1 1/2 pounds baccalà
2 pounds fish carcasses, cut into small pieces, including 1 head
2 cups white wine
1 yellow onion, quartered
4 cloves garlic, chopped
1/4 teaspoon red pepper flakes
1 bay leaf
4 sprigs fresh oregano
2 cups chopped fresh tomatoes
Salt and freshly ground black pepper
2 Cubanelle peppers, chopped
Parsley to garnish

1. Soak the baccalà in water in a large plastic container for 4 days, changing the water once or twice a day.

2. Put the fish carcasses in a big stockpot and cover with water, about 3 quarts. Add the wine, onion, garlic, red pepper flakes, bay leaf, and oregano and bring to a boil. Reduce to a simmer and cook 30 minutes.

3. Strain the soup. Cut the baccalà into bite-size pieces. Add these to the broth, with the tomatoes and Cubanelle peppers. Simmer for 10 minutes. Taste for salt and pepper and serve.

Pasta Fagioli

As my brother-in-law, Jack, said recently, with an appropriate shrug, "Some fazool you eat with a fork, and some fazool you eat with a spoon. It's all good." And it's true; every Italian-American has a different definition of this dish. Sometimes it's soup, sometimes it's pasta. To keep the peace between the two factions, I have been careful to place "fazool" between the soup and pasta recipes. This is my mom's recipe, and I invite you to adjust it to establish your own. But whatever you do, never cover beans when they are boiling. There are gasses emitted that you do not want going back into the pot.

ACTIVE TIME ~ 15 min. TOTAL TIME ~ 1 hr. PORTIONS ~ 4

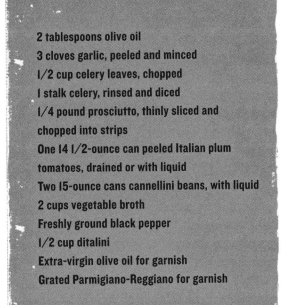

2 tablespoons olive oil

3 cloves garlic, peeled and minced

1/2 cup celery leaves, chopped

1 stalk celery, rinsed and diced

1/4 pound prosciutto, thinly sliced and chopped into strips

One 14 1/2-ounce can peeled Italian plum tomatoes, drained or with liquid

Two 15-ounce cans cannellini beans, with liquid

2 cups vegetable broth

Freshly ground black pepper

1/2 cup ditalini

Extra-virgin olive oil for garnish

Grated Parmigiano-Reggiano for garnish

1. In a saucepan, heat 2 tablespoons olive oil over moderate heat and add the garlic, celery leaves and stalk, and prosciutto. Cook over medium-low heat, stirring occasionally, until the celery is soft, about 7 minutes.

2. Stir in the tomatoes and simmer for 2 minutes. Mix in the beans with the water, broth, and pepper to taste. Raise the heat to high and bring the mixture to boil. Then reduce the heat so the soup is just simmering, and cook until it thickens slightly, 35-40 minutes, stirring occasionally to make sure it doesn't stick to the bottom (if it does, lower the heat).

3. Pour in the ditalini and simmer for about 10 minutes. Then taste the pasta. Keep tasting it, and when it is no longer hard in the center, turn off the heat and serve the soup with a drizzle of extra-virgin olive oil and a sprinkling of Parmigiano-Reggiano.

Pasta

Pasta is a deceptive thing; it is "paste" made with semolina flour and water, shaped and dried. But, really, it is so much more. I cannot imagine life without it. There was not a day that went by in my childhood when I didn't eat pasta. Regardless of what was for dinner, it was always part of the meal. The Italian *primo*, meaning first course, is not a giant bowl of pasta, but a small plate. The biggest meal of the day was usually in the early afternoon, and dinner was much smaller. Here in the United States, families started to eat pasta as the main dinner course. It was easy, quick, and didn't necessarily require a trip to the store. Any of the ingredients for a simple pasta dinner can always be found in the pantry (see Spaghettini Aglio e Olio, page 123).

Pasta makes a great dinner at home, because you can incorporate all the parts of a meal into one bowl: carbohydrates, protein from meat, cheese, fish, or eggs, and vegetables (see Orecchiette with Broccoli Rabe and Sausage, page 137). Of course, dishes like Spaghetti Carbonara (see page 119) originated in Italy, but Italian-Americans have created a lot of the balanced pasta meals we love. During the school week when I was young, we often had pasta with vegetables and then a green salad.

For everyday cooking, dried pasta is a great thing. There are significant differences among brands, mostly in terms of the drying process. The longer pasta dries, the springier it will be when cooked. Artisanal pasta-makers dry in one year what commercial pasta-makers dry in one hour. The result of quick-drying is pasta breaking more often when it is cooked, and not holding its shape well. Another difference among brands is the grade of semolina flour they use. Semolina refers to the part of the wheat used. Bargain brands often use a lower grade, and the pasta has less of a yellow color than superior brands; color alone wouldn't be an issue, but those brands also have inferior taste and texture.

When you make fresh pasta, it is best to do it the day before your meal and let it dry in the freezer overnight. At the very least, dry it for 3 hours, making sure to drape long shapes and separate short ones so you aren't left with one big clump of dough.

All of the recipes on the following pages can be made with fresh or dried pasta, so feel free to substitute dried fusilli for fresh if that works for you, or use your favorite shapes in place of mine. Dried pasta typically

takes heartier, richer, chunkier sauces. Fresh pasta usually goes best with more delicate ones like cream-based (see Fettuccine Alfredo, page 139) or seafood sauces, or simple marinara. Certain shapes, like spaghetti, bucatini, penne, and rigatoni, are simply better dried. Fettuccine, pappardelle, cavatelli, malfatti, fusilli, and gnocchi are usually better fresh. Generally, fresh pasta dough has eggs in it and is therefore better-suited for eating as a main course, but that also makes it richer and more extravagant. My aunt uses eggs in the dough for certain shapes, but not all of them.

People say that pasta, especially fresh pasta, absorbs the sauce it's in. I'm no scientist, but I don't think it's possible for starch to absorb particles of tomato. However, it does absorb water, extracting it from the sauce. My mom's marinara, for example, looks pretty thin on its own. But then she tosses it with fresh pasta in the pot, covers it for a few minutes (not over a flame, but while the pot is still warm), and suddenly, it's thick, coating the pasta perfectly. What has happened is the sauce, which is basically made up of tomato and water, becomes concentrated because some of the water is sucked up by the pasta. So keep in mind that your sauce will become concentrated after it is combined with pasta, and that your pasta will continue to cook during all this.

And what about cooking the pasta? People make it more complicated than it is, and to the detriment of the pasta, by putting oil in the water, rinsing it with cold water, or drizzling it with oil after straining it. To cook a pound of dried pasta, bring 3 quarts of water to a boil. It will boil faster if you keep it covered. When it

just begins to simmer, toss in a big handful of kosher salt, and re-cover it (for fresh pasta, a big pinch will do). The water should be too salty to drink but not unbearably so. It should taste like the sea and will flavor the pasta. Salt raises the boiling point of the water by 6°, which means that it can get hotter before evaporating. If you put the salt in at the beginning, it will just take longer to reach a boil.

Now put the pasta in the water and stir it with a long wooden spoon. The water will stop boiling momentarily because the pasta will lower the temperature. Continue to stir for at least 1 minute. This is the crucial moment when the pasta will stick together if it is allowed to. Once the outer starches have cooked, strands of spaghetti will slide free of one another rather than binding together on contact. After that, stir occasionally. Don't set a timer according to the cooking time as purported on the box. The only way to know when pasta is cooked is to taste it, so keep tasting it after the first 8 minutes or so (fresh pasta cooks in just a few minutes and should be watched until it is done). It should be *al dente*, or "to the tooth," meaning there should be a little bite left in the center, and just a trace of white rawness. Remember, it will continue to cook even after you strain it.

When you strain it, always reserve about a cup of the cooking water. If you don't have a pasta pot with a strainer built in, just use a mug or measuring cup with a handle to scoop out a little water. It will come in handy later if you need to adjust the consistency of the pasta sauce. In Italy, pasta sauce is a *condimenti*, and the proportions are similar to the way we think of condi-ments for burgers and hot dogs, or the way we dress a salad. You only need enough sauce to cling to all the pasta, and you should never see a puddle in the bowl when you're done, as is often the case in American restaurants.

Don't leave the pasta sitting in a colander for half an hour. Shake it to get the excess liquid out, and then pour it right into the pan with your sauce and toss it, ideally just by lifting and shaking the pan over and over. You can also use two wooden spoons or forks, but don't assault your pasta with metal tongs. Trivial as it may seem to compare tossing pasta in a bowl and tossing it in a pan, this is the step that separates good and great pasta. When you move pasta around in a pan with sauce, you emulsify the condiment, the starchy water from cooking the pasta, and the starch in the pasta. Repeated tossing will make this combination thicker, making it really cling to the pasta and coat it, reducing the chances for a puddle to gather.

If you want to further help in thickening your sauce and getting it to really coat the pasta, add a pat of butter to the pasta after draining it. Because butter is made of fat and water, it will emulsify and the sauce will cling and thicken around the pasta. On the other hand, if you drizzle it with oil, which is pure fat, anything that comes in contact with the pasta will slide right off. This is why oil should never be added to the cooking water and why pasta should never be rinsed with water, which removes its surface starch, a precious resource.

Pasta

Mama's Marinara

In culinary school, I learned the term *Mother Sauce*, which refers to a sauce that is the base for other sauces. When I opened Rocco's and was developing the recipes for it, my cooks and I joked that marinara was "Mama Sauce" because it is an ingredient in many other dishes, and of course it's the mother of all sauces. It is also excellent on its own, especially with fresh pasta, which is more porous than dried pasta and therefore grabs the sauce and thickens it. I encourage you to make this in large quantities and keep it on hand in glass or plastic containers. It will keep in your refrigerator for weeks or your freezer for months. Once, when I was a kid, my mother and aunts slathered it all over my back, thinking it would cure "the itchies." I was probably riddled with lice or poison ivy, but whatever it was, they prescribed marinara. At least the trauma of that experience made me forget about the itchies.

ACTIVE TIME ~ 10 min.   TOTAL TIME ~ 1 hr., 25 min.   PORTIONS ~ 6

3 cloves garlic, peeled and crushed

1/2 yellow onion, peeled and chopped fine

3 tablespoons olive oil

Two 28-ounce cans tomato purée

One 28-ounce can crushed tomatoes

I tablespoon tomato paste

I cup chicken broth

I teaspoon sugar

Red pepper flakes to taste

Salt

1. Cook the garlic and onion in the olive oil in a sauce pot over a medium-low flame, about 10 minutes or until garlic is tender and onions translucent, not brown (this is called "sweating" because it will draw out a lot of moisture and flavor).

2. Add all the tomato products. Pour the chicken stock into one of the 28-ounce cans. Fill it the rest of the way with water and add that and the sugar to the pot. Stir and bring to a simmer. Taste and season with red pepper flakes and salt, and cover. Simmer the sauce for about 1 hour. The sauce should be fairly thin but not watery and very smooth. Uncover and simmer for 3 minutes if it is too thin for your taste; add a little water if it seems thick.

Penne alla Vodka

Unlike most Italian-American dishes, which are Southern Italian in origin, this one comes from Tuscany. It is very simple, but the vodka spikes the sauce with a tangy flavor unlike wine or anything else. In Florence, where Penne alla Vodka originated, it is usually very spicy.

ACTIVE TIME ~ 10 min.   TOTAL TIME ~ 40 min.   PORTIONS ~ 4

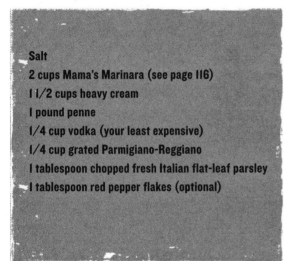

Salt
2 cups Mama's Marinara (see page 116)
1 1/2 cups heavy cream
1 pound penne
1/4 cup vodka (your least expensive)
1/4 cup grated Parmigiano-Reggiano
1 tablespoon chopped fresh Italian flat-leaf parsley
1 tablespoon red pepper flakes (optional)

1. Put a big pot of water over high heat and bring to a boil. Add a handful of salt when it starts to simmer.

2. In a sauce pot over a medium flame, heat up the marinara sauce, then slowly pour in the cream, stirring until uniform. Bring the sauce to a gentle simmer, then lower the heat if necessary, and simmer until it reduces slightly. Add the red pepper flakes.

3. When the water comes to a boil, drop the penne in. When the pasta is almost done, pour the vodka into the sauce and raise the heat slightly. Drain the pasta, reserving about ½ cup of the cooking water. Toss the pasta in the sauce with the Parmigiano-Reggiano, adding a splash of the pasta water if the sauce is very thick. Sprinkle parsley on top and serve.

Spaghetti Scarpariello

I met my friend Antonio Pisaniello in Southern Italy when I was on a research trip, which meant eating my way through the south to find the best food and inspiration (a major perk of being a chef, except that you always return home a little larger than when you left). One day, I went on a wine tour, which usually means you end up drunk, in a cave, spitting out wine and feeling sleepy. But this time, we ended up having lunch prepared by Antonio, the chef at Il Gastronimo. Of the hundred-plus restaurants I ate in on that trip, Antonio cooked the best meal of all, and it included this dish, which he taught me when I invited him to come visit me at Rocco's.

ACTIVE TIME ~ 10 min.   TOTAL TIME ~ 30 min.   PORTIONS ~ 4

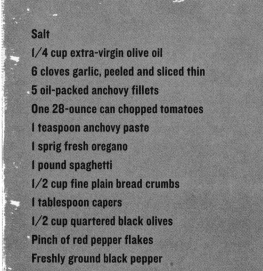

Salt
1/4 cup extra-virgin olive oil
6 cloves garlic, peeled and sliced thin
5 oil-packed anchovy fillets
One 28-ounce can chopped tomatoes
1 teaspoon anchovy paste
1 sprig fresh oregano
1 pound spaghetti
1/2 cup fine plain bread crumbs
1 tablespoon capers
1/2 cup quartered black olives
Pinch of red pepper flakes
Freshly ground black pepper

1. Bring a big pot of water to a boil. When it begins to simmer, add a handful of salt.

2. In a 12-inch skillet over medium heat, warm the olive oil, then add the garlic. Stir until the garlic turns light golden brown. Add the anchovies, breaking them up with the edge of a spoon. Then add the tomatoes, anchovy paste, and oregano. Simmer, stirring constantly, about 3 minutes.

3. When the water comes to a boil, cook the spaghetti, stirring constantly for the first 2 minutes. Drain, reserving 1/2 cup or so of the cooking water.

4. To the skillet, add the bread crumbs, capers, olives, and red pepper flakes. Add the pasta, with cooking water as needed, to the skillet, and toss nonstop about 2 minutes. Season with salt and pepper to taste.

Spaghetti Carbonara

There are so many legends about the inception of this dish, I won't even posit a theory. Some say American soldiers inspired it in Rome during the First World War, some say carbon workers ate it on the job, some say it was named because it had so much black pepper in it that it looked like carbon. Some say it was named by the chef who invented it. All I can be sure of is that this is one of the best pasta dishes ever. I also know that, despite what some people like to think, bacon should not be substituted for the pancetta. Bacon is smoked, while pancetta is just salt-cured, and bacon's smoky taste is overpowering with the egg.

ACTIVE TIME ~ 20 min. TOTAL TIME ~ 35 min. PORTIONS ~ 4

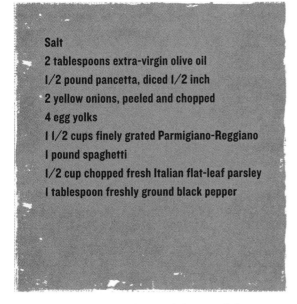

Salt
2 tablespoons extra-virgin olive oil
1/2 pound pancetta, diced 1/2 inch
2 yellow onions, peeled and chopped
4 egg yolks
1 1/2 cups finely grated Parmigiano-Reggiano
1 pound spaghetti
1/2 cup chopped fresh Italian flat-leaf parsley
1 tablespoon freshly ground black pepper

1. Bring a big pot of water to a boil and add salt when it begins to simmer.

2. Heat the olive oil in a large skillet over medium-high heat. When the oil is hot, add the pancetta and cook for 8-10 minutes over a medium flame, until the pancetta has rendered most of its fat but is still chewy and barely browned.

3. Add the onions and cook until they are translucent and soft, about 5 minutes.

4. In a small bowl, slowly whisk about 1/2 cup of the pasta water into the egg yolks, using a fork. This is an important step because if you do not temper the eggs, your sauce will be more like scrambled eggs than creamy carbonara. Add the Parmigiano-Reggiano, parsley, and plenty of freshly ground black pepper, and mix with a fork.

5. Cook the spaghetti till it is al dente and drain it, reserving 1/2 cup or so of water. Transfer it immediately to the skillet with the pancetta and onions. Toss it and turn off the heat.

6. Add the egg mixture to the pan with the pasta and toss all the ingredients to coat the pasta. The sauce should be thick and cling to the spaghetti.

7. Taste the pasta for seasoning and add salt and black pepper, if necessary.

Rigatoni al Ragù

The real name for this sauce, among Italian-Americans, is "Sunday gravy," or simply "gravy." In my family, as in many, we ate this every Sunday, in two courses. After braising all the meat in the marinara sauce, we took it out and ate pasta with the flavor-infused sauce, which also makes plain lasagna special. The meat is typically eaten as the second course.

ACTIVE TIME ~ 25 min. TOTAL TIME ~ 1 hr., 20 min. PORTIONS ~ 4

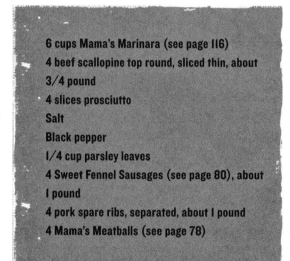

6 cups Mama's Marinara (see page 116)

4 beef scallopine top round, sliced thin, about 3/4 pound

4 slices prosciutto

Salt

Black pepper

1/4 cup parsley leaves

4 Sweet Fennel Sausages (see page 80), about 1 pound

4 pork spare ribs, separated, about 1 pound

4 Mama's Meatballs (see page 78)

1. In a large, deep pot, bring the marinara to a simmer. Meanwhile, pound the scallopine thin and lay them out flat. On each piece, lay a slice of prosciutto, a pinch of salt and pepper, and a few leaves of parsley. Roll each one up fairly tightly and spear with a toothpick to keep them closed. Those are your braciola. Put them into the marinara. Add the spare ribs and cover the pot. Let it simmer for about 1 hour.

2. Meanwhile, sear the sausages on all sides in a large skillet. When the braciola have been simmering for 30 minutes, put a big pot of water on a high heat to boil. 15 minutes later, when the water comes to a boil, add the rigatoni to the water and the sausages to the sauce. Then add the meatballs and simmer for another hour. Remove the meat from the pot, strain the pasta, and toss it in the sauce. Serve together or serve the pasta first and then the meat.

Linguine with Clams

I have taken the liberty of adding pancetta to this popular dish. There is a great precedence for clams and pork together, and it works great in this dish, too. Believe me, the chewy bits of pancetta will be a pleasant surprise, but for Christmas Eve, keep it simple. If you want a red clam sauce, add 1/2 cup of Mama's Marinara (see page 116).

ACTIVE TIME ~ 15 min. TOTAL TIME ~ 40 min. PORTIONS ~ 4

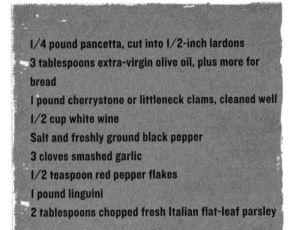

1/4 pound pancetta, cut into 1/2-inch lardons

3 tablespoons extra-virgin olive oil, plus more for bread

1 pound cherrystone or littleneck clams, cleaned well

1/2 cup white wine

Salt and freshly ground black pepper

3 cloves smashed garlic

1/2 teaspoon red pepper flakes

1 pound linguini

2 tablespoons chopped fresh Italian flat-leaf parsley

1. Put the pancetta in a deep skillet and cook over medium heat until the fat has mostly rendered but the pancetta is not yet crisp, about 8–10 min.

2. Bring 3 quarts water to boil in a large stockpot, add salt, and add the linguine, stirring for 1 minute.

3. Add 3 tablespoons of olive oil to the skillet and add the garlic and red pepper flakes. Cook until the garlic is soft and a light golden color, about 10 mins. Add the wine, and bring to a simmer. Add the clams to the skillet and cover. Check every 2–3 minutes for clams that have opened up in the steam and remove them as they do with a slotted spoon. Add the pasta and toss. Garnish with parsley and serve.

Spaghettini with Crab Sauce

Cooking whole crabs slowly in tomato sauce produces a deeply permeated sauce. The shells, like bones in stock, add a lot of flavor and will be removed later. I can't think of Christmas Eve and not think of this crab sauce. I like it a little hot and recommend serving it with extra red pepper flakes on the table.

ACTIVE TIME ~ 20 min. TOTAL TIME ~ 1 hr., 40 min. PORTIONS ~ 4

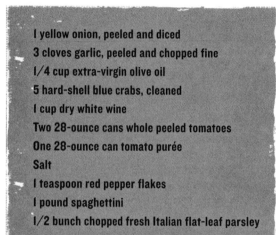

1 yellow onion, peeled and diced

3 cloves garlic, peeled and chopped fine

1/4 cup extra-virgin olive oil

5 hard-shell blue crabs, cleaned

1 cup dry white wine

Two 28-ounce cans whole peeled tomatoes

One 28-ounce can tomato purée

Salt

1 teaspoon red pepper flakes

1 pound spaghettini

1/2 bunch chopped fresh Italian flat-leaf parsley

1. Sauté the onion and garlic in the olive oil in a stockpot till translucent, about 10 minutes. Add the crabs, cover, and cook for 15-20 minutes, stirring occasionally. Add the wine. Bring the liquid to a low simmer. Add all the tomatoes and simmer for about 1 hour.

2. Season with salt and red pepper flakes to taste. Remove the whole crabs and any pieces of shell. Strain if necessary.

3. Boil the pasta in plenty of salty water and drain, retaining 1 cup or so of the cooking water. Toss the pasta with the sauce, adding a splash of water if it seems too thick. Sprinkle the parsley on top and serve.

Spaghettini Aglio e Olio

While the rest of the family was eating spicy crab sauce with our spaghettini, my cousin Angela, who detests fish of any kind, in any form, always ate hers with oil and garlic. But before you think "poor little Angela," try making this old standby my mother's way: smashing the garlic cloves but leaving them whole flavors the olive oil while adding a sweet meatiness to the dish. The garlic is tender and mild. This is also the base for several other simple dishes; you can add any vegetable you like. My favorites are spaghetti squash, spinach, and broccoli rabe.

ACTIVE TIME ~ 5 min. TOTAL TIME ~ 30 min. PORTIONS ~ 4

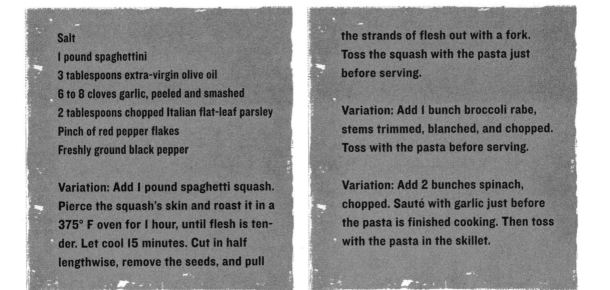

Salt

I pound spaghettini

3 tablespoons extra-virgin olive oil

6 to 8 cloves garlic, peeled and smashed

2 tablespoons chopped Italian flat-leaf parsley

Pinch of red pepper flakes

Freshly ground black pepper

Variation: Add I pound spaghetti squash. Pierce the squash's skin and roast it in a 375° F oven for I hour, until flesh is tender. Let cool 15 minutes. Cut in half lengthwise, remove the seeds, and pull the strands of flesh out with a fork. Toss the squash with the pasta just before serving.

Variation: Add I bunch broccoli rabe, stems trimmed, blanched, and chopped. Toss with the pasta before serving.

Variation: Add 2 bunches spinach, chopped. Sauté with garlic just before the pasta is finished cooking. Then toss with the pasta in the skillet.

1. Place a big pot of water over high heat and add a handful of salt. When it begins to simmer, add the spaghettini and stir well for the first 2 minutes.

2. While the pasta cooks, heat the olive oil in a 10-inch sauté pan over medium. Add the garlic and cook until it is golden brown, smashing it with edge of a spoon as it cooks, about 6 minutes. When the garlic is light brown, remove the pan from the heat and add the parsley and red pepper flakes. Drain the pasta and add it to the sauté pan. Toss, season with salt and pepper, and serve immediately.

Penne with White Pesto

Everybody loves pesto, but most people don't realize that the term refers to a variety of sauces, all containing nuts and garlic puréed together. It is not necessarily green. This pesto is made with walnuts rather than pignoli, and has ricotta. I like to use penne rigate, which has little ridges like a ribbed shirt, because the pesto settles in those grooves.

ACTIVE TIME ~ 10 min.   TOTAL TIME ~ 25 min.   PORTIONS ~ 4

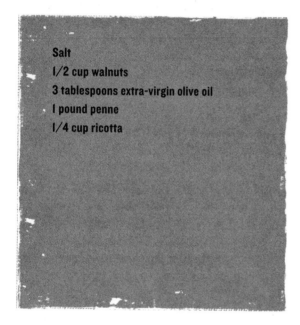

Salt
1/2 cup walnuts
3 tablespoons extra-virgin olive oil
I pound penne
1/4 cup ricotta

1. Preheat the oven to 325° F. Put a big pot of water over high flame. Add a handful of salt when it begins to simmer.

2. Toss the walnuts in a bowl with I tablespoon of the olive oil and a pinch of salt. Spread them out on a baking sheet and toast in the oven for about 10 minutes. Remove the pan and set the walnuts aside to cool.

3. Cook the penne till al dente. Drain the pasta, retaining 1/2 cup or so of the cooking water.

4. Chop the nuts and mix them with the ricotta, remaining 2 tablespoons of olive oil, and a pinch of salt if you like. Toss the pasta with the pesto, adding a splash of water if it seems too thick. It should be thick and creamy.

Farfalle with Grilled Sausage, Fennel, and Baby Artichokes

Farfalle is bow tie–shaped pasta. It is perfect in dishes like this, with the fairly large chunks of meat and vegetable involved. Fennel, sausage, and artichokes are such a happy combination.

ACTIVE TIME ~ 25 min.   TOTAL TIME ~ 1 hr.   PORTIONS ~ 4

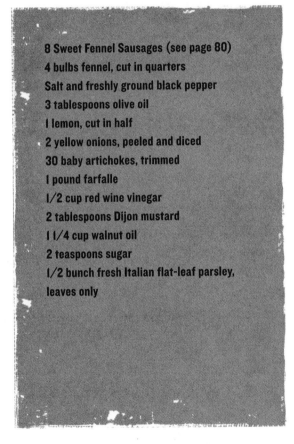

8 Sweet Fennel Sausages (see page 80)

4 bulbs fennel, cut in quarters

Salt and freshly ground black pepper

3 tablespoons olive oil

I lemon, cut in half

2 yellow onions, peeled and diced

30 baby artichokes, trimmed

I pound farfalle

1/2 cup red wine vinegar

2 tablespoons Dijon mustard

I 1/4 cup walnut oil

2 teaspoons sugar

1/2 bunch fresh Italian flat-leaf parsley, leaves only

1. Heat a grill or grill pan on medium-high. Cook the sausages until they are done, turning them to prevent burning. Set them aside. Season the fennel with salt and pepper, brush with olive oil, and grill until brown and tender. When cool enough to handle, slice the sausages on the bias into 1/4-inch slices, and cut the fennel into similarly-sized pieces. Keep the sausages and fennel warm while you prepare the rest of the dish.

2. Bring a large pot of water to a boil for the pasta and add 2 teaspoons salt. In a separate, large pot of water, add lemon, onion, 1 teaspoon salt, and 1/4 teaspoon pepper, and bring to a boil. Add trimmed artichokes and top with a small plate to hold them beneath the surface of the water. Cook until the hearts are almost completely tender, about 15 minutes. Remove the artichokes from the pot and pat dry. Season them with salt and pepper to taste, and grill for 5 minutes. Set them aside in a warm place and cut in half when cool enough to handle.

3. Add the pasta to the boiling water and cook al dente. In a medium bowl, whisk together the vinegar and mustard. Slowly whisk in the walnut oil until emulsified. Mix in 1 teaspoon salt, sugar, and 1/4 teaspoon pepper. Toss the fennel, sausages, artichokes, and pasta with the walnut vinaigrette, and top with whole parsley leaves. Serve immediately.

Bucatini with Anchovies

When Sicilians talk about this dish, they never mention the *finocchio* (fennel) that makes it special. Dating from early medieval times, this classic Sicilian recipe is delicious when made with the right ingredients—that's the secret—which are sometimes difficult to find outside the Mediterranean region.

ACTIVE TIME ~ 15 min. TOTAL TIME ~ 30 min. PORTIONS ~ 4

Salt

2 heads fennel, halved, cored, and thinly sliced

2 medium sweet white onions, thinly sliced

3 tablespoons extra-virgin olive oil

1 pound dry bucatini

15 large anchovies (in oil), 4 finely chopped, the rest whole

1 tablespoon saffron threads, soaked in warm water

2 tablespoons currants

2 tablespoons pine nuts

1 teaspoon sugar

Freshly ground black pepper

1. Bring a big pot of water to boil over high heat and add a handful of salt when it begins to simmer.

2. Meanwhile, in a large sauté pan, sweat the fennel and onions in 2 tablespoons of the olive oil, cover, and cook until the vegetables are translucent and tender throughout. While the onions and fennel cook, add the bucatini to the boiling water and cook until al dente, stirring occasionally. When the pasta is 2 minutes away from being done, add the chopped anchovies to the cooked fennel and onions. Cook until the fish is warm, about 2 minutes. Remove the sauté pan from the heat and stir in the saffron, currants, pine nuts, and sugar. Add the remaining 1 tablespoon of olive oil.

3. Add the pasta, with about 1/4 cup of the cooking water, to the pan with the fennel, anchovy, currants, and pine nuts, and toss and serve.

Nicolina's Lasagne

My mother always made lasagna on Christmas Day. It is simple and easy to make. She swears she doesn't like meat in lasagna and that hers is plain, but her secret is to use the marinara in which meatballs, braciola, and sausages have been simmered for a ragù. We eat the meat separately, but the flavor is imparted to the sauce and therefore the whole lasagna, and often there were little bits of meatball hiding in there. My friends used to skip their own family plans and come to my house if lasagna was on the menu.

ACTIVE TIME ~ 15 min. TOTAL TIME ~ 50 min. PORTIONS ~ 4

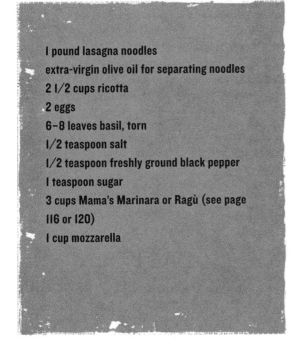

I pound lasagna noodles

extra-virgin olive oil for separating noodles

2 1/2 cups ricotta

2 eggs

6–8 leaves basil, torn

1/2 teaspoon salt

1/2 teaspoon freshly ground black pepper

I teaspoon sugar

3 cups Mama's Marinara or Ragù (see page 116 or 120)

I cup mozzarella

1. Preheat the oven to 375° F.

2. Cook the noodles in heavily salted boiling water, stirring constantly for the first 2 minutes. Drain them when they are still slightly undercooked because when the lasagna is baked, they will cook more. Drizzle a little olive oil over the noodles and separate them. Otherwise, they will stick together and tear.

3. In a separate bowl, combine the ricotta, eggs, basil, salt, pepper, and sugar.

4. Ladle enough marinara to coat the bottom of a glass casserole 13 x 9 x 2 or similar size. Lay down noodles to cover the bottom of the casserole. Add a layer of the ricotta mixture. Repeat. Make 3 layers, total. Top with any remaining marinara and the mozzarella.

5. Bake for about 20 minutes, just long enough to melt the mozzarella and heat the lasagna throughout.

Spaghetti Primavera

Primavera means "spring." Although this dish can feature any number of fresh vegetables, to me fava beans are the ultimate spring ingredient. They are in season very briefly, but during that time, I try to eat them as much as possible.

ACTIVE TIME ~ 5 min. TOTAL TIME ~ 30 min. PORTIONS ~ 4

Salt
4 cloves garlic, peeled and thinly sliced
1/4 pound cremini or halved white button mushroom caps, about 12, quartered
1/2 pound asparagus, cut into 1-inch pieces and blanched
2 carrots, peeled, sliced on the bias, and blanched
1/2 pound fava beans, shelled and blanched
1 tablespoon minced fresh Italian flat-leaf parsley
Freshly ground black pepper
1 pound spaghetti
Parmigiano-Reggiano, grated

1. Put a big pot of water over high heat and bring to a boil. Add a handful of salt when it begins to simmer.

2. Heat the oil in a skillet over medium heat. Add the garlic and cook until it is slightly brown, about 3 minutes. Add the mushrooms and cook until they are soft, about 5 minutes. Add the other vegetables and the parsley to warm through and finish cooking. Season with salt and pepper to taste. Keep warm.

3. Cook the spaghetti al dente. Drain, reserving about 1/2 cup or so of the cooking water. Add the pasta, with the reserved cooking water as needed, to the pan with the vegetables, toss all the ingredients nonstop for 2 minutes, and serve with Parmigiano-Reggiano.

Most of us think of fresh pasta as a very labor-intensive thing, but my immigrant relatives, even now, think nothing of spending an afternoon rolling out cavatelli (also known as "gabba-deel") or fusilli. My aunt Elena is superhumanly adept at producing large quantities of pasta in short periods of time, and I hired her at Rocco's to do just that and to teach my cooks her skills. It is not hard to learn, though it takes some practice to form the shapes at lightning speed. She has been practicing for some time. In fact, when my uncles Davide and Silvio, on a mission to find Uncle Joe a wife, showed up at Elena's house in Flumeri in 1967 to convince her to give them a picture of her to send to him in New York, they found her sitting at the kitchen table, rolling hundreds of fusilli. Perhaps that was the moment they knew she was the one for Joe. By the way, they took a picture, somewhat against Elena's will, and sent it to Joe, who immediately began writing her love letters and married her about two months later. He has been gladly eating fusilli ever since.

Homemade pasta is an excellent option for special occasions, and a fun project, especially with a friend or your kids. It is best to make the dough and shape it the night before, letting it dry in the fridge overnight.

Remember that fresh pasta cooks much faster than dry. A good rule is to take it out of the boiling water as soon as it floats to the top. Fresh pasta is a lot less forgiving than dry pasta, and goes from perfect to overcooked very quickly. To have total control, you might want to cook it in batches. Drain it as you do dry pasta, retaining some of the cooking water. Then toss it in the pan with whatever sauce you have made.

Fresh Pasta

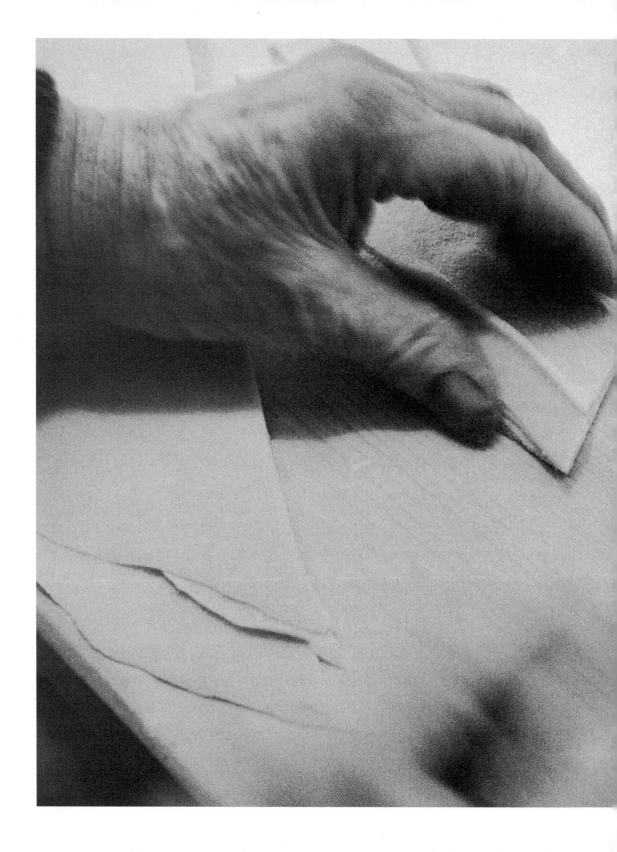

Pasta Dough and Shapes

ACTIVE TIME ~ 45 min.   **TOTAL TIME** ~ 45 min.   **PORTIONS** ~ 1 1/4 pounds each

Fusilli and Orecchiette

1/2 cup all-purpose flour

1/2 cup "double zero" flour

1/4 cup semolina flour

Pinch of salt

I egg

1/4 cup hot tap water

Linguine "al'Uovo"

1/2 cup all-purpose flour

1/2 cup "double zero" flour

1/4 cup semolina flour

2 eggs

Pinch of salt

Cavatelli

1/2 cup all-purpose flour

1/2 cup "double zero" flour

1/4 cup semolina flour

Pinch of salt

1/2 cup hot tap water

Fettuccine and Pappardelle

1/2 cup all-purpose flour

1/2 cup "double zero" flour

1/4 cup semolina flour

Pinch of salt

I egg

1/3 cup hot tap water

For all pasta doughs:
Combine flour and salt in a mound. Create a well in the center. Crack eggs/pour water into the well. Stir the wet ingredients into the dry, gradually incorporating all the flour with your fingers. When the dough comes together, knead for several minutes, until it's smooth, not sticky. Shape it according to the directions below.

Fusilli: Pull off small handfuls of dough. Roll each into a rope about 1/8 inch thick. Cut them into 2-inch pieces. Position a thin metal or wood dowel at a 45°angle to one piece. (My aunt uses the straight edge of a coat hanger.) Roll the dowel over the pasta. It should curl around the dowel (to make a spiral/corkscrew shape). Push it off and repeat.

Orecchiette: Pull off small handfuls of dough. Roll each into a rope about 1/4 inch thick. Cut them into 1/2-inch pieces. Push your pointer or middle finger down into each piece of dough, rotating against the work surface to stretch and thin it out. You will have a little finger-hat. Touch that finger to your thumb and turn the orecchiette inside-out, onto your thumb.

Cavatelli: Pull off small handfuls of dough. Roll each into a rope about 1/8 inch thick. Cut them into 2-inch pieces. Place your three middle finger-tips down behind one piece of dough and roll them over it (towards you) making three indents and curving the pasta slightly.

Fettuccine/Linguine/Pappardelle: These shapes are made most easily with a pasta machine. Otherwise, roll the dough out as thin as possible. Flour the surface generously and roll the dough up with as little air inside as possible. With a sharp knife, cut strips across the short side, 1/4-inch wide for fettuccine, 1/2 inch for pappardelle, or as thin as possible for linguine. Spread out the noodles to dry so they don't stick or tangle.

Manicotti

These manicotti are not made of pasta; they are a light, delicate crepe and they are very special.

ACTIVE TIME ~ 30 min. TOTAL TIME ~ 45 min. PORTIONS ~ 8

Crepes:

1 egg

3/4 cup whole milk

1/2 cup water

1/4 cup club soda

1/2 tablespoon sugar

Pinch of salt

1 1/4 cups all-purpose flour, sifted

3 tablespoons unsalted butter, melted

1. In a large bowl, whisk the egg just until the whites and yolks are blended. Pour in the milk, water, and club soda, and stir. Add the sugar and salt. Whisk in the sifted flour, blending until the mixture is smooth. Stir in the melted butter.

2. In a hot, lightly buttered, very shallow nonstick (ideally flat) pan, about 6 inches in diameter, spoon enough batter to very thinly coat the pan. Move the pan slowly to spread the batter out evenly. Leave the pan over medium-low heat until the bottom browns slightly and can be flipped. Use a spatula to flip the crepe. It should be paper-thin. Remove the crepe from the pan and lay it flat to cool.

Filling:

1 pound ricotta

1 cup diced fresh mozzarella

1 cup grated Parmigiano-Reggiano

1/2 bunch fresh basil, chopped

1/2 bunch fresh Italian flat-leaf parsley, chopped

2 teaspoons salt

2 teaspoons freshly ground black pepper

1 teaspoon sugar

1. Combine all the ingredients well.

2. With the manicotti flat on your work surface, spoon a heaping tablespoon onto each crepe, in a strip about 1 inch away from the edge. Roll up each crepe from the filled side to the other side. Lay seam-side down to keep closed.

3. Serve with marinara sauce.

Fusilli Pomodorini

Cherry and grape tomatoes, when thrown into a hot skillet, blister and burst and ooze a thick liquid that clings to pasta perfectly. I like to cook the tomatoes so they are very blistered on the skin and just beginning to burst but not yet broken down, because of the texture they give the dish. If you want to create more of a sauce, cover the tomatoes and they will pop open.

ACTIVE TIME ~ 10 min. TOTAL TIME ~ 40 min. PORTIONS ~ 4

Salt

2 tablespoons extra-virgin olive oil

2 cloves garlic, peeled and smashed

1 pint grape or cherry tomatoes

Pinch of red pepper flakes

1 1/4 pound fresh fusilli

1/4 cup diced fresh mozzarella (optional)

2 anchovy fillets, chopped (optional)

1/4 cup grated Parmigiano-Reggiano (optional)

Freshly ground black pepper

3/4 cup fresh basil leaves, torn

1. Bring a big pot of water to boil and add a handful of salt when it begins to simmer.

2. Starting with a cold skillet, add the olive oil and slowly sweat the garlic over low heat, until it is very soft and sweet, not browned, about 10 minutes. Add the tomatoes and red pepper flakes to the skillet. Turn the heat up slightly and let the tomato skins blister. But keep an eye on the skillet—the garlic should remain soft and light in color, about 15 minutes.

3. Meanwhile cook the pasta in the boiling water, stirring constantly for the first 2 minutes. Drain, reserving about 1/4 cup of the cooking water separately. Add the pasta, with the reserved cooking water, to the pan with the pomodorini and toss all the ingredients nonstop for 2 minutes. At this point, toss in the mozzarella and/or anchovies, or simply serve with Parmigiano-Reggiano. Taste and season with salt and black pepper and top with basil leaves.

Orecchiette with Broccoli Rabe and Sausage

This is one of many examples from Italian cuisine of the love affair between bitter greens and pork. There are examples from all over the world, but I feel safe in saying Italians do it best.

ACTIVE TIME ~ 30 min.   TOTAL TIME ~ 50 min.   PORTIONS ~ 4

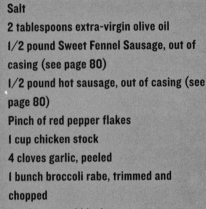

Salt
2 tablespoons extra-virgin olive oil
1/2 pound Sweet Fennel Sausage, out of casing (see page 80)
1/2 pound hot sausage, out of casing (see page 80)
Pinch of red pepper flakes
1 cup chicken stock
4 cloves garlic, peeled
1 bunch broccoli rabe, trimmed and chopped
Freshly ground black pepper

1. Heat the olive oil in a large skillet over high heat. Add the sweet and hot sausage and break it into bite-size pieces with a spatula or a spoon as it browns on all sides. Add the red pepper flakes.

2. Bring a big pot of water to a boil. Add a handful of salt when it begins to simmer.

3. When the sausage is nicely browned, pour in the chicken stock. This is deglazing—the liquid will pick up all the tasty bits of meat stuck to the bottom of the pan. As it simmers, scrape the bottom of the skillet with the edge of a wooden spoon to help the process along. It will take 2 or 3 minutes. Lower the heat when most of the liquid has evaporated. Add the garlic cloves to the pan and let them brown slowly. With a fork or the edge of a spoon, smash the garlic cloves, and move them around to brown all sides. Add the broccoli rabe and let it simmer, uncovered, about 6 minutes, or until broccoli rabe is tender, but not mushy, and bright green.

4. Pour the orecchiette into boiling water and stir. If, when the broccoli rabe is cooked, there is excess liquid in the pan, remove the broccoli rabe and continue to simmer the chicken stock until it has reduced and thickened enough to cling to the pasta.

5. Drain the pasta, reserving some of the cooking water separately. Add the pasta, incorporating a few tablespoons of the reserved cooking water if needed, to the pan with the broccoli rabe and sausage, toss repeatedly, and serve.

Linguine Puttanesca

Puttanesca means "in the style of the whore." Don't worry, this sauce will not reflect badly on you. Legend says that this was a popular sauce among prostitutes because its ingredients were cheap and it was easy to whip up between "customers." Well, it has overcome its own reputation; while it is undeniably cheap, it also has class and a whole lot of taste.

ACTIVE TIME ~ 10 min. TOTAL TIME ~ 40 min. PORTIONS ~ 4

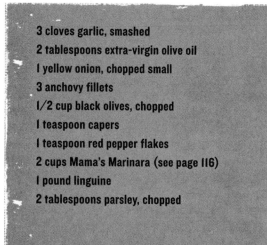

3 cloves garlic, smashed

2 tablespoons extra-virgin olive oil

1 yellow onion, chopped small

3 anchovy fillets

1/2 cup black olives, chopped

1 teaspoon capers

1 teaspoon red pepper flakes

2 cups Mama's Marinara (see page 116)

1 pound linguine

2 tablespoons parsley, chopped

1. In a large skillet over medium-low heat, sauté the onions and garlic in the olive oil until soft, about 10 minutes.

2. Bring a big pot of water to boil over high heat. When it begins to simmer, add a handful of salt.

3. Add the anchovies, olives, capers, and red pepper flakes (adjust to fit your taste, but this is traditionally a hot dish). Simmer for about 10 minutes. The anchovies will break down and melt into nothing, and the flavors will mingle.

4. Add the marinara sauce to the skillet and stir. Meanwhile, cook the linguine and drain, reserving about 1/2 cup of the cooking water. Toss the pasta in the skillet with the sauce and parsley. Add a few tablespoons of the reserved cooking water to adjust the consistency if necessary.

Fettuccine Alfredo

When you've had a really bad day, this is the ultimate Italian-American indulgence. But remember, a moment on the lips, a lifetime on the hips.

ACTIVE TIME ~ 15 min. TOTAL TIME ~ 1 hr., 20 min. PORTIONS ~ 4

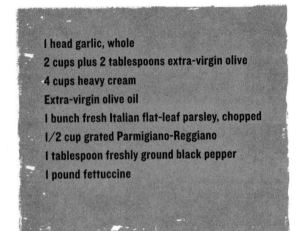

I head garlic, whole

2 cups plus 2 tablespoons extra-virgin olive

4 cups heavy cream

Extra-virgin olive oil

I bunch fresh Italian flat-leaf parsley, chopped

1/2 cup grated Parmigiano-Reggiano

I tablespoon freshly ground black pepper

I pound fettuccine

1. Preheat the oven to 350° F.

2. Cut the very top off the whole head of garlic and submerge it in 2 cups of olive oil in a sauce pot. Cover the pot with foil and bake in the oven for 45 minutes. Check that the garlic is very soft and tender. If it is not, recover with foil, return to the oven, and check again in 15 minutes. If the garlic is tender, remove the foil and bake for another 15 minutes, until brown. Remove the pot from the oven. Let the garlic cool for a few minutes.

3. Meanwhile, in a small sauce pot, heat the heavy cream over a low flame. Bring it to a low simmer and reduce it by half. Remove the pot from the heat. This is called double cream.

4. Squeeze all of the garlic cloves out of their peels, using a spoon if it is still very hot, and put the garlic in a blender with a few spoons of the oil in which it was roasted. Add just enough oil to get the blender going. Add 2 tablespoons of water and purée.

5. Meanwhile, bring a big pot of salted water to a boil.

6. Put the pan with the double cream back over a medium-low flame and whisk in the roasted garlic purée, chopped parsley (most but not all; reserve a few pinches), Parmigiano-Reggiano, and black pepper.

7. Boil the fettuccine. When the pasta is cooked al dente, drain and toss it with the alfredo sauce. Sprinkle with the reserved parsley and serve.

Linguine with Calamari

My aunt Elena makes stuffed calamari with linguine, but I think she's the only one who can get it right. I love the texture of the big whole squids swimming in long pasta strands. Also, the calamari taste is prevalent in the sauce because they cook together.

ACTIVE TIME ~ 20 min.   TOTAL TIME ~ 45 min.   PORTIONS ~ 4

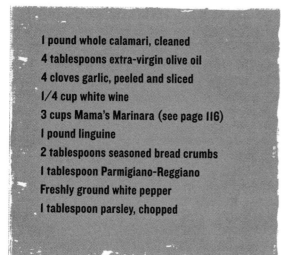

I pound whole calamari, cleaned

4 tablespoons extra-virgin olive oil

4 cloves garlic, peeled and sliced

1/4 cup white wine

3 cups Mama's Marinara (see page 116)

I pound linguine

2 tablespoons seasoned bread crumbs

I tablespoon Parmigiano-Reggiano

Freshly ground white pepper

I tablespoon parsley, chopped

1. Pull the heads off the calamari. Finely chop the heads. Set aside.

2. Heat the olive oil in a medium stockpot and sauté the garlic over medium-low heat for about 5–6 minutes. Meanwhile, bring water to a boil in a large pot.

3. Add the squid to the garlic. Turn up the heat to medium and deglaze the pan with the white wine. When the wine reduces a little, add the marinara sauce. Simmer 10 minutes, stirring.

4. When the water boils, cook the pasta. Drain the pasta, reserving 1/2 cup or so of the cooking water.

5. Toss the pasta in the sauce, adding the bread crumbs, Parmigiano-Reggiano, and herbs.

Pappardelle Bolognese

Pappardelle is an extra-wide, flat, long noodle, similar to fettuccine but wider. It is most traditionally paired with meaty tomato sauces, often ragù. When we decided to include it on the menu at Rocco's, neither I nor any of my cooks had a recipe for Bolognese. Naturally, we turned to my mother. She didn't have a particular recipe either, but on the first try, she created the perfect Bolognese to match this shape of pasta. This is peasant food, so don't be surprised that the ratio of meat to sauce is low. A little bit of meat goes a long way in sauces like this.

ACTIVE TIME ~ 20 min. TOTAL TIME ~ 1 hr., 20 min. PORTIONS ~ 4

1/8 pound ground veal	2 cups Mama's Marinara (see page 116)
1/8 pound ground beef	2 cups chicken stock
1/8 pound ground pork	Salt and red pepper flakes
3 tablespoons extra-virgin olive oil	1/4 cup grated Parmigiano-Reggiano
2 carrots, peeled and diced	1 1/4 pound pappardelle
4 stalks celery, rinsed and diced	Salt
1 yellow onion, peeled and diced	Pepper
1 glass red wine	

1. In a stockpot, over high heat, brown the meat in the olive oil. Lower the heat and add everything else, except the pasta and the cheese, cover, and simmer 1 hour.

2. Meanwhile, bring a big pot of water to a boil. Add a handful of salt when it begins to simmer. Cook the pasta in salted boiling water, drain, and toss it in the pot with the sauce. Taste and season with salt and pepper. Serve with the Parmigiano-Reggiano.

Risotto is thought to be only a Northern Italian dish, but in fact, white arborio rice has been consumed in Sicily since the middle ages, being imported from Lombardy and Piedmont. Cooking risotto is a transcendental process and requires more focus and attention than any other Italian dish. That said, I still recommend it to home cooks. It simply requires extreme patience, and time to master the gentle finesse that lets you know exactly when to add more liquid, and how much. It's the shortest love affair you'll ever have. It's just cooked rice, and yet it is incredibly special. Risotto rice comes from the Po Valley in Northern Italy and has a high starch content, which, when it's cooked slowly, creates the silky, creamy coating you just can't coax out of Uncle Ben's. The cooking process is a symbiotic give-and-take of starch and liquid. The rice absorbs the flavor in the liquid, and the starch thickens the liquid. You are beating it up to get that starch, which is why you have to stir it nonstop, but, as mobsters say, don't leave any marks. The risotto must be in its original shape in the end, not beaten into mush. I have included a risotto recipe for every season, but feel free to eat them whenever they appeal to you, and to experiment with your own versions.

Risotto

Risotto Milanese

This bright yellow risotto is the most famous of any in America. It is incredibly simple. The color and flavor come from saffron, the most expensive spice in the world (don't worry, you will use a teeny amount). If risotto were a woman, this is the lean, intense beauty, the Katharine Hepburn of risottos, with defined cheekbones, a faint Chanel No. 5 scent, and a lot of power over me. Sautéed chicken liver is wonderful on top of this one. This is a sunny, summer risotto.

ACTIVE TIME ~ 25 min. TOTAL TIME ~ 45 min. PORTIONS ~ 4

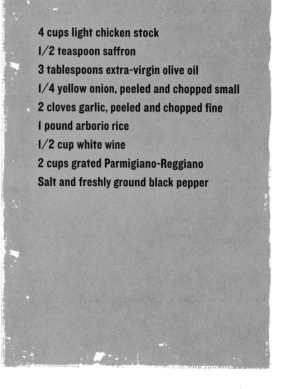

4 cups light chicken stock

1/2 teaspoon saffron

3 tablespoons extra-virgin olive oil

1/4 yellow onion, peeled and chopped small

2 cloves garlic, peeled and chopped fine

I pound arborio rice

1/2 cup white wine

2 cups grated Parmigiano-Reggiano

Salt and freshly ground black pepper

1. In a stockpot, bring the chicken stock to a boil, then lower to a simmer. Add 1 thread of saffron, wait a few minutes to taste, and then add more. (The flavor is released gradually, so if you put it all in at once, it may be too strong, and a waste.) Once the flavor is infused but not overpowering, turn off the heat and leave the stock uncovered. If you think the saffron flavor has gotten too strong, add some water, 1 cup at a time, then turn off the heat.

2. In a stockpot over low heat, add the olive oil and sauté the onion and garlic until they turn translucent. Add the rice and cook for 2-3 minutes to harden the outer starch. It will get shiny and translucent. Add the wine and bring to a simmer while stirring, then begin adding the chicken stock, about 1 cup at a time, until the rice is cooked and creamy. Stir constantly and evenly while the stock is being absorbed for the creamiest rice. The rice is cooked when it is tender throughout but not mushy, about 20 minutes. Remove the pan from the heat and allow the risotto to stand for a few minutes to absorb any remaining liquid. Just before serving, mix in the Parmigiano-Reggiano and season to taste with salt and pepper.

Risotto Verde

This is a spring day risotto. You could use any leafy greens you like, such as chard or kale, and experiment with herbs. If you like the taste of pesto, this will be similar but so much better.

ACTIVE TIME ~ 25 min. TOTAL TIME ~ 45 min. PORTIONS ~ 4

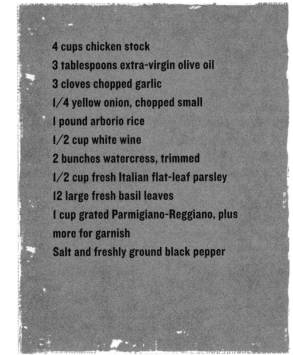

4 cups chicken stock

3 tablespoons extra-virgin olive oil

3 cloves chopped garlic

1/4 yellow onion, chopped small

1 pound arborio rice

1/2 cup white wine

2 bunches watercress, trimmed

1/2 cup fresh Italian flat-leaf parsley

12 large fresh basil leaves

1 cup grated Parmigiano-Reggiano, plus more for garnish

Salt and freshly ground black pepper

1. In a stockpot, bring the chicken stock to a boil, then turn off the heat and leave the pot uncovered.

2. In a large sauté pan over low heat, add 1 tablespoon of olive oil and sauté the garlic and onion until it turns translucent, 7–8 minutes. Add the rice and cook for 2-3 minutes to harden the outer starch. Add the wine and bring to a simmer while stirring, then begin adding the chicken stock, about 1 cup at a time, until the rice is cooked and creamy. Stir constantly and evenly while the stock is being absorbed for the creamiest rice. The rice is cooked when it is tender throughout but not mushy, about 20 minutes.

3. Meanwhile, in a pot of boiling water, blanch the watercress for 30 seconds, drain, and put directly into an ice bath to "shock" it. Blend the watercress, parsley, and basil with 2 tablespoons olive oil in a blender or with an immersion blender. Add this to the risotto at the last minute and stir to evenly incorporate into the risotto. Remove the pan from the heat, mix in the Parmigiano-Reggiano, and season to taste with salt and pepper.

Risotto ai Funghi

This risotto should taste and smell like playing in autumn leaves, embracing fall. If you can't find truffle butter, don't substitute truffle oil. It will be delicious with the mushrooms alone.

ACTIVE TIME ~ 20 min. TOTAL TIME ~ 40 min. PORTIONS ~ 4

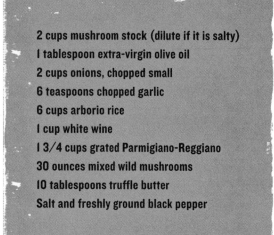

2 cups mushroom stock (dilute if it is salty)

1 tablespoon extra-virgin olive oil

2 cups onions, chopped small

6 teaspoons chopped garlic

6 cups arborio rice

1 cup white wine

1 3/4 cups grated Parmigiano-Reggiano

30 ounces mixed wild mushrooms

10 tablespoons truffle butter

Salt and freshly ground black pepper

1. In a stockpot, bring the mushroom stock to a boil, then turn off the heat, leaving the stock uncovered on the stovetop.

2. In a large sauté pan over low heat, add the olive oil and sauté the onions and garlic until they turn translucent. Add the rice and cook for 2-3 minutes to harden the outer starch. Add the wine and bring to a simmer while stirring, then begin adding the stock, about 1 cup at a time, until the rice is cooked and creamy. Stir constantly and evenly while the stock is being absorbed for the creamiest rice. The rice is cooked when it is tender throughout but not mushy. Remove the pot from the heat and allow the risotto to stand for a few minutes to absorb any remaining liquid. Just before serving, mix in the Parmigiano-Reggiano, and season to taste with salt and pepper.

Caesar Salad, p. 206

Verdure Room Temperature, p. 198

Mama's Meatballs, p. 78

Eggplant Rollatini, p. 76

Mixed Antipasto

Chopped Mixed Salad, p. 204

Porterhouse alla Mama, p. 184

Stuffed Artichokes, p. 82

Risotto Bolognese

Although Italians would shoot you for it, you can make regular risotto and then finish it off with some Bolognese sauce. Over there, of course, they would start by making a stock from the meat in the Bolognese. But we're here now. This is comforting, stick-to-your-ribs winter risotto.

ACTIVE TIME ~ 20 min. **TOTAL TIME** ~ 40 min. **PORTIONS** ~ 4

2 quarts light beef stock

2 quarts light chicken stock

I tablespoon extra-virgin olive oil, plus more for garnish

1/2 onion, chopped small

2 cloves garlic, peeled and minced

I pound arborio rice

1/2 cup white wine

2 cups Bolognese sauce (see page 141; make half that recipe)

2 cups grated Parmigiano-Reggiano

Salt and freshly ground black pepper

1. In a stockpot, bring both stocks to a boil together, then turn off the heat, leaving the pot uncovered on the stovetop.

2. In a large sauté pan over low heat, add 1 tablespoon of olive oil and sauté the onions and garlic until they turn translucent. Add the rice and cook for 2-3 minutes to harden the outer starch. Add the wine and bring to a simmer while stirring, then begin adding the stock, about 1 cup at a time, until the rice is cooked and creamy. Stir constantly and evenly while the stock is being absorbed for the creamiest rice. The rice is cooked when it is tender throughout but not mushy, about 20 minutes. Remove the pan from the heat and allow the risotto to stand for a few minutes to absorb any remaining liquid. Just before serving, mix in the Bolognese sauce and the Parmigiano-Reggiano, and season to taste with salt and pepper.

The purchasing and cooking of fish have changed since the days when fishermen would push a cart with the catches of the day into small Italian towns where women would buy whole fish. It was usually served whole, too, usually just with olive oil, salt, and lemon. In America, we tend to first lay eyes on our fish many steps away from the sea. Especially in supermarkets, filleted fish is king. My family hardly ate any seafood in Italy, because their town is in the mountains, so it was in America that they incorporated it into their diet.

We kids succeeded at convincing our elders to stay away from whole fish for the most part, being wary of the heads. We kids all ate fillets of salmon and a lot of shrimp in my house, while my father would eat a whole trout. My mother and aunts also got a lot of their fish flavors from preserved fish like anchovies, sardines, and baccalà (salt cod). But what never changed was the fact that fish is almost always prepared very simply. Try combining olive oil, sea salt, and lemon juice and applying it, like a dipping sauce, to any grilled or baked fish. I've also included a dozen great recipes.

Pesce

Grilled Trout, Porgy, or Sea Bass

If you leave the heads on your fish while they cook, they will be much more tasty, I swear. Simple grilled fish is one of my favorite dinners, especially in the summer, and especially if I can sit outside while I eat it. Have a small barbeque and try it, even if you are compelled to cut off the fish heads before serving your guests.

ACTIVE TIME ~ 5 min. TOTAL TIME ~ 20 min. PORTIONS ~ 4

Four 6-ounce whole trout, porgy, or sea bass, heads still on
2 lemons, sliced thin
4 sprigs fresh rosemary

4 sprigs fresh thyme
2 tablespoons extra-virgin olive oil
Salt and freshly ground black pepper

1. Slice the fish down the front, from top to bottom. Stuff each with 2 thin slices of lemon and a sprig each of rosemary and thyme. Brush with the olive oil, season to taste with salt and pepper, and grill, about 7 minutes on each side or until the flesh is opaque and juicy.

Salmon with Cucumber Salad

This is an extremely easy dish to make at home. Salmon and cucumber are a great match, especially in the summer. The crisp cucumber cuts the oil in the fish.

ACTIVE TIME ~ 10 min. TOTAL TIME ~ 20 min. PORTIONS ~ 4

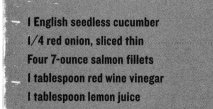

1 English seedless cucumber
1/4 red onion, sliced thin
Four 7-ounce salmon fillets
1 tablespoon red wine vinegar
1 tablespoon lemon juice

2 tablespoons extra-virgin olive oil plus more to rub on salmon
Salt and freshly ground black pepper
15 leaves fresh Italian flat-leaf parsley

1. Preheat the broiler.

2. To make the salad: peel the cucumber and cut it in half lengthwise, scoop out the middle with a spoon, and discard. Cut the cucumber into 1/4-inch slices. Combine with all the other ingredients, except the salmon, in a bowl.

3. Rub or brush the salmon with olive oil and sprinkle with salt and pepper.

4. Broil the salmon for about 4 minutes on one side, then flip and cook for about 1 minute on the other for medium rare. Serve with the cucumber salad.

Broiled Octopus

I'm no scientist, but I can tell you from experience that the old myth that boiling octopus in water with a cork in it really does tenderize the flesh. I can't tell you why, but I suggest you try it. Octopus became more prevalent in my mother's kitchen as I got older. The first time my finicky sister, Maria, saw it, she had wandered into the kitchen to find a pot bubbling away on the stove. Out of habit, she took the top off to see what it was. When she saw the "suction cups," as she calls them, she ran, literally screaming, out of the room. A couple of years later, she met her now-husband Jack's parents for the first time. Unfortunately, they served octopus.

ACTIVE TIME ~ 15 min. TOTAL TIME ~ 2 hr. PORTIONS ~ 4

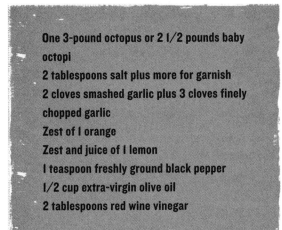

One 3-pound octopus or 2 1/2 pounds baby octopi

2 tablespoons salt plus more for garnish

2 cloves smashed garlic plus 3 cloves finely chopped garlic

Zest of 1 orange

Zest and juice of 1 lemon

1 teaspoon freshly ground black pepper

1/2 cup extra-virgin olive oil

2 tablespoons red wine vinegar

1. Boil the octopus in a large pot of water with 2 tablespoons of salt and 2 cloves of smashed garlic with a cork for 1 hour and 20 minutes. Drain the octopus and shock in an ice bath. Drain it well and cut the tentacles into 3-inch chunks. (If you are using babies, leave them whole.)

2. To make the marinade, combine the chopped garlic, lemon juice and zest, orange zest, a pinch of salt, pepper, olive oil, and vinegar. Pour this and the octopus into a large Ziploc bag and marinate at room temperature for 30 minutes. Preheat your broiler.

3. Broil the octopus until it gets slightly charred, about 3 minutes on each side. Taste for salt and serve.

Shrimp Scampi

In Italian, the name of this dish would be translated "Shrimp Shrimp," which is some proof that it has been renamed over here. *Scampi* is shrimp, but to Americans, it refers to the whole shrimp (head-on). The first time I saw shrimp scampi outside of my house, I was working in an Italian restaurant called Centurion in Garden City, New York. They cooked everything on sizzle platters or in aluminum "to go" containers. The owner, Rocky, had a slight gambling problem and controlled portion sizes according to how he was doing. So sometimes the shrimp scampi, even though the menu said "jumbo shrimp," was made with small shrimp. They were cooked in the pizza oven in an aluminum container with corn oil and garlic and parsley. Not very appealing. The next time I saw them was in a place called Fernwood, a resort in the Catskills where I worked during culinary school to make some extra money. They used to take frozen blocks of peeled and deveined shrimp, basically cover them with butter, and let them sit on the stove all night, just scooping them out as they needed them. Clearly, I do not recommend either of these methods. Don't be scammed. Try this one.

ACTIVE TIME ~ 10 min. TOTAL TIME ~ 40 min. PORTIONS ~ 4

3 tablespoons extra-virgin olive oil

Zest of 1 lemon

1 clove garlic, peeled and chopped

6 to 8 leaves fresh oregano, chopped or 1/2 tablespoon dried

24 jumbo shrimp

4 slices Italian bread (see page 217)

Salt and freshly ground black pepper

Sauce:

3 cloves garlic, peeled and chopped fine

2 tablespoons extra-virgin olive oil

1 tablespoon fresh chopped oregano

2 tablespoons fresh lemon juice

3 tablespoons unsalted butter

Salt and freshly ground black pepper

1. Preheat the broiler.

2. Make a marinade: combine the olive oil, lemon zest, garlic, and oregano in a wide, shallow dish or a casserole. Marinate the shrimp for 30 minutes, then broil the shrimp and the bread. Broil 1 minute each side.

3. In a small sauté pan, sauté the garlic in the oil. Add the oregano and lemon juice. Remove the pan from the heat. Add the butter, and season to taste with salt and pepper.

4. Drizzle the sauce over the shrimp. Serve with the bread to mop up the sauce.

Stewed Baccalà

This is another Christmas Eve recipe. There's something so elegant about the red peppers and tomatoes with the mild but hearty salt cod.

ACTIVE TIME ~ 20 min. TOTAL TIME ~ 4 days, 45 min. PORTIONS ~ 4

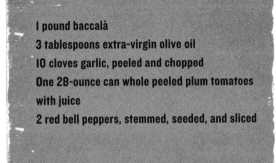

I pound baccalà

3 tablespoons extra-virgin olive oil

10 cloves garlic, peeled and chopped

One 28-ounce can whole peeled plum tomatoes with juice

2 red bell peppers, stemmed, seeded, and sliced

1. Submerge the salt cod in cold water in a large container and soak in the refrigerator for 4 days, changing the water once or twice each day.

2. Heat the olive oil in a sided skillet over medium-low heat. Add the garlic and stir until tender and light golden, about 5 minutes. Add the tomatoes and peppers and gently simmer for about 20 minutes, or until the tomatoes start to break down. Drain the baccalà. Cut the baccalà into big chunks and add it to the skillet. Stir to combine all the ingredients. Cover the pot and simmer for 15 minutes, then serve.

Red Snapper and Heirloom Tomatoes Poached in Olive Oil

I came up with this idea while brainstorming for a show on the Food Network called *Melting Pot*. I was trying to think of ways to bridge the flavors my family cooked with with new ideas of how to prepare them. Poaching in olive oil makes for an extremely tasty and tender fish. At Union Pacific, I have long used the method of poaching in different kinds of fat, and for a simple dish like this, olive oil is the best choice because it imparts more flavor than anything else.

ACTIVE TIME ~ 15 min. TOTAL TIME ~ 35 min. PORTIONS ~ 4

2 quarts olive oil

Four 6-ounce red snapper fillets, skin on

1 teaspoon salt

1/4 teaspoon freshly ground black pepper

4 heirloom tomatoes

1/4 pound slab bacon, cut into thick lardons

2 cloves garlic, peeled and sliced thin

3 cups packed spinach

1. Warm the olive oil in a large pot. Season the fish with the salt and pepper. Submerge the fillets in the oil. Add the tomatoes and submerge them. Cook slowly until the fish is done, about 15 minutes. Remove the fish.

2. In a sauté pan over medium-high heat, cook the lardons until crispy. Remove and reserve the lardons and pour out most of the fat. Add the garlic to the sauté pan and cook until it is slightly brown. Add the spinach and cook until it is wilted.

3. Remove the pan from the heat and keep warm. Add the fish and crisp skin. Serve the fish with the tomatoes atop the spinach and sprinkle with the lardons.

Seared Tuna with Basil Oil

When I was sixteen, I made basil oil for all of my relatives for Christmas, because I was really excited about food and, also, I was broke. It is the only way to preserve basil, aside from in a can of tomatoes, and it is excellent for instant flavoring on anything—pasta, eggs, chicken, and so forth—when you haven't really planned out dinner.

ACTIVE TIME ~ 25 min. TOTAL TIME ~ 35 min. PORTIONS ~ 4

Salt

2 cups packed fresh basil leaves

I cup plus I teaspoon olive oil

Four 6-ounce sashimi-grade tuna steaks

1/4 teaspoon freshly ground black pepper

Zest of I lemon

1. Bring 4 quarts of water to boil in a stockpot and add 3 tablespoons salt. Set up an ice bath. Blanch the basil for 2 minutes in the boiling water, then transfer it immediately to the ice bath. Cool the basil for 2 minutes, drain, then squeeze any excess water from the basil.

2. Blend the basil and 1 cup of the olive oil in a blender until well mixed. Strain through a coffee filter into a small bowl.

3. Heat a cast-iron skillet over high heat until it is very hot. Season the tuna with 1 teaspoon of salt and the pepper. Brush the tuna lightly with 1 teaspoon of olive oil. Place the steaks in the hot pan and cook until the bottom is brown and crusty, about 3 minutes. Flip the tuna and cook for 1 minute. (The tuna will be just seared on the outside and raw in the middle.) Remove the steaks to a plate. Drizzle with the basil oil and garnish with lemon zest.

Oil and Vinegar Bass in a Pouch

The inspiration for this dish was to take it down to its essential elements. It's a great combination of the sweet and sour flavors I love, and best of all, it can be made with almost no cleanup. You can use whatever vegetables are in season and appeal to you.

ACTIVE TIME ~ 20 min. TOTAL TIME ~ 40 min. PORTIONS ~ 4

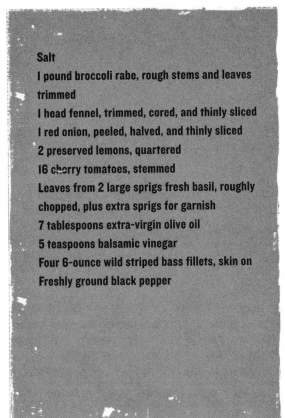

Salt
1 pound broccoli rabe, rough stems and leaves trimmed
1 head fennel, trimmed, cored, and thinly sliced
1 red onion, peeled, halved, and thinly sliced
2 preserved lemons, quartered
16 cherry tomatoes, stemmed
Leaves from 2 large sprigs fresh basil, roughly chopped, plus extra sprigs for garnish
7 tablespoons extra-virgin olive oil
5 teaspoons balsamic vinegar
Four 6-ounce wild striped bass fillets, skin on
Freshly ground black pepper

1. Preheat the oven to 375° F.

2. Bring a large stockpot of water to boil and add 2 tablespoons of salt. Set up an ice bath. Cook the broccoli rabe in the boiling water until it is bright green and tender, about 4 minutes. Drain, cool in the ice bath, and drain again. Set the broccoli rabe aside.

3. Lay four 12-inch pieces of foil out on a counter. Put the fennel, onion, lemons, tomatoes, and chopped basil in a medium bowl, and season with salt and pepper to taste. Drizzle with 1 tablespoon of olive oil and 1 teaspoon of balsamic vinegar. Pile a mound of vegetables on each sheet of foil. Season the fish on both sides with salt and pepper to taste, and place on top of the vegetables. Drizzle each pile with 1 tablespoon of olive oil and 1 teaspoon of balsamic vinegar, and use a second piece of foil to seal the pouch completely.

4. Put the pouches on a baking sheet and cook in the oven for 6 minutes. Turn the package over and continue baking for 6 more minutes. While the fish cooks, sauté the broccoli rabe in a large sauté pan with 2 tablespoons of olive oil until it is hot throughout. Season with salt and pepper to taste. To serve, put each pouch on a plate and open the pouches at the table. Garnish with basil sprigs and pass the broccoli rabe.

Seafood alla Griglia

There is nothing much better than a charred piece of fish with a little lemon juice squeezed onto it. And there's something about the openness of a grill that always encourages me to combine lots of different meats or fishes. That's the way my family has always barbequed. Why have one thing if you can have four or five?

ACTIVE TIME ~ 25 min. TOTAL TIME ~ 45 min. PORTIONS ~ 4

9 lemons

9 pounds of assorted Mediterranean fish, such as branzino, dorade, and red mullet, scaled and gutted, and shellfish, like langoustine and large sea scallops, shelled

Extra-virgin olive oil, for dressing the fish

Salt and freshly ground black pepper

4 ounces fresh thyme sprigs

10 sprigs fresh Italian flat-leaf parsley, roughly chopped

1. Preheat a grill.

2. Juice 5 of the lemons and cut the other 4 in half.

3. Rinse the fish inside and out and pat dry. Place the fish and shellfish in a shallow plate and sprinkle on all sides with the lemon juice. Drizzle olive oil over everything and season to taste inside and out with salt and pepper. Stuff the whole fish with a few thyme sprigs.

4. When the grill is too hot to hold your hand 6 inches above for more than a few seconds, it's ready. Grill the fish without moving it until golden brown grill marks appear. Turn it over and finish grilling on the second side until moist and opaque. Some fish may take longer than others; check often and remove the fish as they reach their individual doneness.

5. To serve, arrange the cooked fish on a large serving platter and drizzle all over with extra-virgin olive oil. Mix any leftover lemon juice with olive oil and sea salt to make a dipping sauce. Garnish with the parsley and lemon halves.

Broiled Lobster Tails

This is the main event on Christmas Eve. It is a fancy though simple dish and my relatives get giddy about it. My aunt Elena serves it with melted butter on the side. My uncle Joe likes to brag about finding the biggest lobster tails—sometimes the tail alone is a pound. These go great with broccoli rabe.

ACTIVE TIME ~ 15 min. TOTAL TIME ~ 30 min. PORTIONS ~ 4

4 large lobster tails, about 9 ounces each
3 tablespoons extra-virgin olive oil
Juice of 1 large lemon or 2 small lemons
Salt and freshly ground black pepper

1. Heat the broiler.

2. Cut the lobster shells with scissors down the underside from north to south and pull the meat out, reserving the shells. Line up the tails on the broiler rack sheet and place the meat on top of them. Drizzle the meat with the olive oil and lemon juice. Sprinkle with a few pinches of salt and pepper, and broil for 15 minutes.

This much-maligned dish is one of the greatest things to come out of the Italian-American kitchen. I have long been convinced that the world is divided between people who love parmigiana and people who lie. My mother made chicken, veal, and eggplant parmigiana with some regularity when I was young, and my brother, sister, and I were always ecstatic when she did. This is not a dish she learned from her mother or in Italy. My mom taught herself how to make it from eating it in Italian-American restaurants. Like meatballs, there are a lot of parmigianas out there, and my mom's recipe far surpasses the average. Her trick is to layer it like a lasagna. Making several thin layers creates a lighter parmigiana than one typically encounters. Don't hold back on the mozzarella when you get to the top, however. That's the other trick.

Parmigiana

Eggplant Parmigiana

Slice the eggplant thick for this one; it will give the parmigiana structure and meatiness. If the eggplant is too thin, it will break down to mush when it is baked. Of all the newfangled parmigianas out there, like turkey, sausage, onion, bread, and shrimp parmigiana, and the classics I have here, this may be my favorite. There's something in the chemistry between the eggplant and the mozzarella that is like heaven.

ACTIVE TIME ~ 25 min. TOTAL TIME ~ 55 min. PORTIONS ~ 6

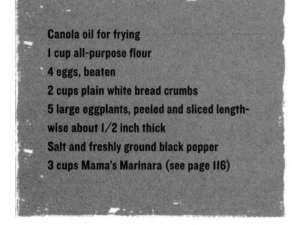

Canola oil for frying
I cup all-purpose flour
4 eggs, beaten
2 cups plain white bread crumbs
5 large eggplants, peeled and sliced lengthwise about I/2 inch thick
Salt and freshly ground black pepper
3 cups Mama's Marinara (see page 116)

6 tablespoons grated Parmigiano-
Reggiano, plus extra for garnish
I pound mozzarella, diced
3 tablespoons chopped fresh basil, plus
extra for garnish
3 tablespoons chopped fresh Italian
flat-leaf parsley

1. Heat the canola oil in a large, heavy pot.

2. Preheat the oven to 375° F.

3. Salt the eggplant. Spread the slices out on a cookie sheet or on several paper towels and salt both sides generously. Let them sit for about 10 minutes. Then wipe off the excess salt with a paper towel.

4. Meanwhile, place the flour, eggs, and bread crumbs in separate shallow dishes and arrange them in that order.

5. Fill a deep, heavy stockpot 1/3 of the way up with canola oil and set over high heat.

6. Dredge each slice of eggplant in the flour, then in the eggs, then in the bread crumbs, and then carefully place them in the hot oil. Fry the slices until golden brown. Remove the eggplant from the oil and place the slices on a cookie sheet or paper towels to drain any excess oil. Season them with salt and pepper to taste on both sides.

7. Heat the marinara in a sauce pot or the microwave. Spoon about 1/2 cup or enough just to cover bottom into the bottom of a large glass or other ovenproof casserole.

8. Lay down one even layer of eggplant in the marinara. Then layer 2 tablespoons Parmigiano-Reggiano, 1/2 cup diced mozzarella, 1/2 cup marinara, pinch of basil, 1 pinch of parsley, pinch of salt, and pepper. Then place another layer of eggplant and repeat the layering process.

9. Make 3 layers total. The top should be sauce and both cheeses, but no herbs. Bake for about 20 minutes. The cheese should melt nicely, but only begin to brown at the edges.

10. Remove from the oven and sprinkle with basil and Parmigiano-Reggiano. Serve hot.

Chicken Parmigiana

Chicken "parm" is such a classic, people take it for granted. A lot of people pound the chicken extremely thin, but I find that too-thin chicken gets very dry very easily. I like to bite into a tender, moist piece of chicken.

ACTIVE TIME ~ 15 min. TOTAL TIME ~ 40 min. PORTIONS ~ 6

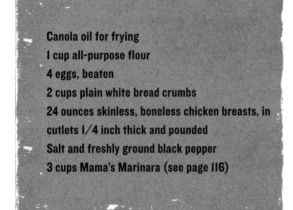

Canola oil for frying
1 cup all-purpose flour
4 eggs, beaten
2 cups plain white bread crumbs
24 ounces skinless, boneless chicken breasts, in cutlets 1/4 inch thick and pounded
Salt and freshly ground black pepper
3 cups Mama's Marinara (see page 116)

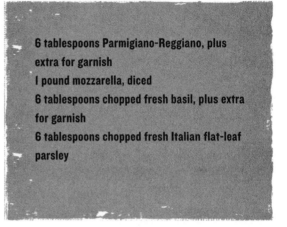

6 tablespoons Parmigiano-Reggiano, plus extra for garnish
1 pound mozzarella, diced
6 tablespoons chopped fresh basil, plus extra for garnish
6 tablespoons chopped fresh Italian flat-leaf parsley

1. Heat the canola oil in a large, heavy pot.

2. Preheat the oven to 375° F.

3. Meanwhile, place the flour, eggs, and bread crumbs in separate shallow dishes and arrange them in that order.

4. Dredge each slice of chicken in the flour, then in the eggs, then in the bread crumbs, and then carefully place them in the hot oil. Fry the chicken until golden brown. Remove the chicken from the oil and place it on paper towels to drain any excess oil. Season the chicken with salt and pepper to taste on both sides.

5. Spoon about 1/2 cup into the bottom of a large glass or other ovenproof casserole.

6. Lay down one even layer of chicken in the marinara. Then layer 2 tablespoons Parmigiano-Reggiano, 1/2 cup diced mozzarella, 1/2 cup marinara, pinch of basil, pinch of parsley, pinch of salt, and pepper. Then place another layer of chicken and repeat the layering process.

7. Make 3 layers total. The top should be sauce and both cheeses, but no herbs. Bake for about 20 minutes. The cheese should melt nicely, but only begin to brown at the edges.

8. Remove from the oven and sprinkle with basil and Parmigiano-Reggiano. Serve hot.

Veal Parmigiana

As much as I like eggplant and chicken in parmigiana to be sliced thick, I love veal to be pounded as wispy thin as possible, and dressed lighter. Skip the tomato sauce and squeeze a little lemon juice over the finished dish.

ACTIVE TIME ~ 15 min. TOTAL TIME ~ 40 min. PORTIONS ~ 6

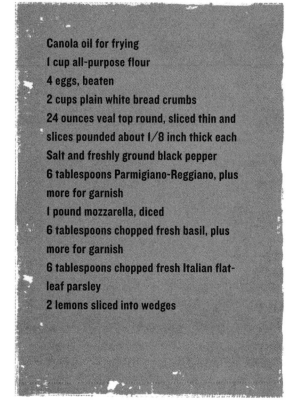

Canola oil for frying

I cup all-purpose flour

4 eggs, beaten

2 cups plain white bread crumbs

24 ounces veal top round, sliced thin and slices pounded about 1/8 inch thick each

Salt and freshly ground black pepper

6 tablespoons Parmigiano-Reggiano, plus more for garnish

I pound mozzarella, diced

6 tablespoons chopped fresh basil, plus more for garnish

6 tablespoons chopped fresh Italian flat-leaf parsley

2 lemons sliced into wedges

1. Heat the canola oil in a large, heavy pot.

2. Preheat the oven to 375° F.

3. Meanwhile, place the flour, eggs, and bread crumbs in separate shallow dishes and arrange them in that order.

4. Dredge each slice of veal in the flour, then in the eggs, then in the bread crumbs, and then carefully place them in the hot oil. Fry the veal until golden brown. Remove the veal from the oil and place it on paper towels to drain any excess oil. Season the veal with salt and pepper to taste on both sides.

5. Lay down one even layer of veal in the marinara. Then layer 2 tablespoons Parmigiano-Reggiano, 1/2 cup diced mozzarella, pinch of basil, pinch of parsley, salt, and pepper. Then place another layer of veal and repeat the layering process.

6. Make 3 layers total. The top should be sauce and both cheeses, but no herbs. Bake for about 20 minutes. The cheese should melt nicely, but only begin to brown at the edges.

7. Remove from the oven and sprinkle with basil and Parmigiano-Reggiano. Serve with lemon wedges.

As I went through my adolescence, I became more and more convinced that I was growing up in the care of mountain men. Some of the family activities, especially at my grandmother's house, which is now my uncle Joe's house, seemed quite wild. I was, after all, a city kid, and every time I wandered outside, it seemed like my uncles were clubbing something over the head and skinning it. In fact, I was shocked when I saw my mom once deep in the process of removing feathers from a small bird. Not her most glamorous moment. There was the occasional live pig in the backyard, and rabbits and pigeons were a constant presence. Uncle Joe, the butcher, sometimes went to a farm in New Jersey to purchase an entire cow, which he butchered there. He still hunts deer and proudly brings it home for dinner during the hunting season. There were always, and still are, dozens of sausages hanging in the garage. For us, meat was expensive, but my family found ways to keep it available.

Carne

Chicken with Chunky Lemon Sauce

I must admit that I "adapted" this one from the great chicken with lemon sauce at Rao's, the legendary East Harlem hot spot that I loved, though I could never get in. Well, partly *because* I could never get in.

ACTIVE TIME ~ 25 min.   TOTAL TIME ~ 45 min.   PORTIONS ~ 4

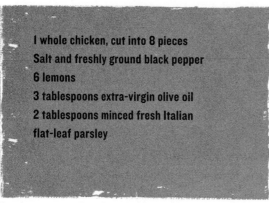

I whole chicken, cut into 8 pieces
Salt and freshly ground black pepper
6 lemons
3 tablespoons extra-virgin olive oil
2 tablespoons minced fresh Italian flat-leaf parsley

1. Preheat the broiler.

2. Place the chicken pieces on a broil pan. Season on all sides with salt and pepper. Broil for about 20 minutes, or until the chicken is almost entirely cooked through and golden brown, making sure to turn the pieces now and then so they do not burn.

3. Slice off the top and bottom ends of 3 lemons, so that they can stand up on a cutting board. Using a sharp knife, remove the peel and pith in a downward motion, revealing the flesh of the lemon underneath. Work the knife in between the membranes to get to the individual lemon sections. Set the segments aside in a bowl. Squeeze out the juice from the leftover skins. Juice the remaining 3 lemons into the same bowl. Add the olive oil, parsley, 1 teaspoon of salt, and 1/4 teaspoon of pepper.

4. Once the chicken is just about cooked through, remove it from the oven and cover it with the lemon sauce. Return the pan to the broiler and cook for 5 more minutes. Remove the chicken from the oven, and transfer it to a large platter. Serve right away.

Pollo Sotto Mattone

This is originally a Tuscan dish, but it has made its way all over Italy. Originally, it would have been cooked in a terra-cotta pot with a heavy top, which weighted the chicken down, pushing the skin against the hot stone and therefore making it very crisp. A terra-cotta pot works great if you have one, but a cast-iron skillet is just fine.

ACTIVE TIME ~ 15 min. TOTAL TIME ~ 40 min. PORTIONS ~ 2-3

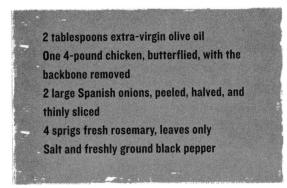

2 tablespoons extra-virgin olive oil
One 4-pound chicken, butterflied, with the backbone removed
2 large Spanish onions, peeled, halved, and thinly sliced
4 sprigs fresh rosemary, leaves only
Salt and freshly ground black pepper

1. Preheat oven to 450° F. Wrap 2 bricks in heavy-duty tinfoil if you have them. You can use 2 cast-iron skillets instead.

2. Heat a large cast-iron skillet over a medium-high heat and add the olive oil. Add the chicken to the skillet, skin side down. Weigh down the chicken with the bricks or skillets. It should flatten out, maximizing the crispy skin surface area.

3. The skin will brown quickly, 4-5 minutes. Lower the heat to medium-low and cook for about 8 minutes more. Carefully turn the chicken over; if it sticks, do not pull it. Let it continue cooking until it easily releases. The chicken should still be tender to the touch (cooked about halfway), very crispy, and dark golden brown.

4. Brown the underside of the chicken for about 5 minutes, then put back skin-down. Add the onions and rosemary to the pan around and on top of the chicken. Transfer the skillet to the oven and bake until the onions are caramelized and the chicken is cooked through, about 10 minutes.

5. Remove the chicken from the pan and let it rest for 10 minutes. Meanwhile, transfer the skillet to the stove and cook the onions down over medium heat. Any liquid should reduce and the onions should become very soft and sweet. Serve around the chicken.

Persimmon Squab

I've been eating persimmon my whole life. In Italian, they're called *kaki*. I love the bright, tart, but sweet flavor of ripe persimmons, but they are so hard to find in season. The fuyu type in particular is almost never ripe. Recently, I learned that if you cook the hychia type, they become incredibly sweet. So my persimmon predicament is a thing of the past. The first time I saw a persimmon tree, I was in Tuscany. It was nighttime and I was walking outside when I saw red glowing Christmas ornaments, just hanging in midair, or so it seemed. It was truly stunning. When I got closer, I realized that the red balls were the persimmons. In fact, persimmon trees were the inspiration for Christmas trees.

ACTIVE TIME ~ 5 min. TOTAL TIME ~ 30 min. PORTIONS ~ 4

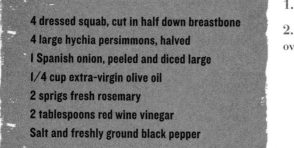

4 dressed squab, cut in half down breastbone

4 large hychia persimmons, halved

I Spanish onion, peeled and diced large

1/4 cup extra-virgin olive oil

2 sprigs fresh rosemary

2 tablespoons red wine vinegar

Salt and freshly ground black pepper

1. Preheat the oven to 350° F.

2. Throw all of the ingredients in a pan and roast in the oven for 30 minutes.

Grilled Pekin Duck with Chestnuts and Wine

Everyone thinks cooking duck is so "gourmet," but this dish was inspired by the simplicity of my family's food. Ingredients that we all love happen to come together really well here.

ACTIVE TIME ~ 25 min. TOTAL TIME ~ 1 hr. PORTIONS ~ 4

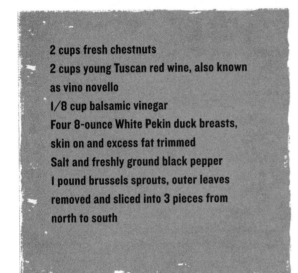

2 cups fresh chestnuts

2 cups young Tuscan red wine, also known as vino novello

1/8 cup balsamic vinegar

Four 8-ounce White Pekin duck breasts, skin on and excess fat trimmed

Salt and freshly ground black pepper

1 pound brussels sprouts, outer leaves removed and sliced into 3 pieces from north to south

1. To skin the chestnuts, score them with an *X* on their flat sides and cook them in a pot of boiling water until the outer shells peel back. Drain the chestnuts and remove the peels with a paring knife.

2. In a small saucepan, combine the wine and vinegar and reduce by half over medium heat. Add the chestnuts and cook until they are tender, about 10 minutes. Set aside.

3. Heat a heavy-bottomed sauté pan over medium heat, and season the duck on both sides with salt and pepper. Sauté the duck breasts slowly, skin side down, draining the fat that accumulates in the pan into a bowl. Reserve the fat.

4. Add 2 tablespoons of the duck fat to the chestnuts. Swirl to combine, and adjust the seasoning with the salt and pepper to taste.

5. When the fat has rendered off the duck breasts and the skin is golden brown and crispy, turn them over and cook for 2 or 3 minutes on the second side for medium-rare meat. Remove from heat and keep warm.

6. Drain all but 1 tablespoon of the fat from the pan and increase the heat to high. Add the brussels sprouts and cook until they are golden brown and tender. Season them to taste with salt and pepper.

7. To serve, pile some brussels sprouts in the center of each plate. Slice each duck breast into 5 pieces and lay them on top of the greens. Scatter some of the chestnuts about and drizzle the dish with the wine reduction.

Baby Lamb Chops Scottaditto

When we were kids, we almost never ate lamb chops, which were expensive. We had pork chops every week, but lamb was reserved for the baby lamb (see page 175) or leg of lamb (see page 176) on Easter. There were a few times, however, when our grandmother made lamb chops for us just because she knew we all loved them. *Scottaditto* means "finger-blistering." These lamb chops are so delicious, you will not be able to wait for them to cool down to eat them. And it is totally acceptable to pick them up because they are little.

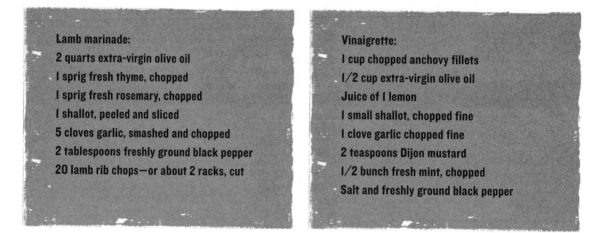

ACTIVE TIME ~ 20 min.   **TOTAL TIME** ~ 2 days 20 min.   **PORTIONS** ~ 4

Lamb marinade:

2 quarts extra-virgin olive oil

1 sprig fresh thyme, chopped

1 sprig fresh rosemary, chopped

1 shallot, peeled and sliced

5 cloves garlic, smashed and chopped

2 tablespoons freshly ground black pepper

20 lamb rib chops—or about 2 racks, cut

Vinaigrette:

1 cup chopped anchovy fillets

1/2 cup extra-virgin olive oil

Juice of 1 lemon

1 small shallot, chopped fine

1 clove garlic chopped fine

2 teaspoons Dijon mustard

1/2 bunch fresh mint, chopped

Salt and freshly ground black pepper

1. Mix together all of the marinade ingredients in a Ziploc bag and add the chops. Marinate the chops for at least 2 full days in the refrigerator.

2. Remove the chops from the marinade and scrape off any solids, then grill the chops to medium rare, about 2 minutes on each side. The oil will cause the flames to rise, which is the goal—the outsides should be charred, the fat somewhat rendered, and the inside just hot throughout and very juicy.

3. Combine all of the vinaigrette ingredients and drizzle it over the lamb chops before serving.

Baby Lamb Brodettato

This quick-braise is a perfect winter dish. The result is a tender, rich, tight stew. *Brodedatto* means "little broth." And the cool part, to me at least, is that it is enriched with egg yolks, a technique people always attribute to the French. It turns out the Italians are just as clever with their eggs. So there.

ACTIVE TIME ~ 20 min.   TOTAL TIME ~ 50 min.   PORTIONS ~ 6

1 1/2 lemons

3 pounds lamb from the shoulder and leg

Salt and freshly ground black pepper

3 tablespoons extra-virgin olive oil

1 tablespoon unsalted butter

2 slices parma ham, shredded

1 onion, finely chopped

1/8 cup all-purpose flour

1 cup white wine

3 egg yolks

Leaves from 2 sprigs fresh marjoram, roughly chopped

Leaves from 2 sprigs fresh Italian flat-leaf parsley, roughly chopped

1 pound wide egg noodles, tossed in 2 tablespoons unsalted butter

1. Zest half of 1 lemon and juice both halves. Reserve the half lemon.

2. Cut the lamb into 1 1/2-inch pieces and pat it dry. Rub the lamb with the half lemon, and season it to taste with salt and pepper.

3. In a large pan with a tight-fitting lid, heat the oil and butter over medium heat until foaming, then add the lamb and ham. Cook, stirring occasionally, until the lamb pieces begin to brown, then add the onion and continue to cook until the lamb is nicely browned all over.

4. Sprinkle over the flour and stir to coat all the lamb. Lower the heat and add the wine, then cover and simmer for 30 minutes, or until the lamb pieces are fork-tender.

5. In a small bowl, beat together the egg yolks, lemon zest, lemon juice, and the marjoram. When the lamb is ready, slowly add the yolks to the pan, whisking constantly. The sauce should be thickened and smooth. Garnish with the parsley and serve right away.

Roast Leg of Lamb

Everyone thinks Italians eat lamb only on Easter. As a matter of fact, my family sometimes eats it a few times in a week. This is a great cut because it is inexpensive and there is hardly any work to be done. It also happens to be delicious. Just throw everything together, marinate, and then roast. And if you start with it frozen, it can double as dinner/disappearing evidence in a homicide, as in the wickedly funny Alfred Hitchcock short *Lamb to the Slaughter*.

ACTIVE TIME ~ 15 min. TOTAL TIME ~ 1 day 3hr. 40 min. PORTIONS ~ 4

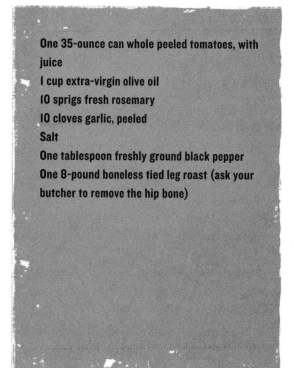

One 35-ounce can whole peeled tomatoes, with juice

1 cup extra-virgin olive oil

10 sprigs fresh rosemary

10 cloves garlic, peeled

Salt

One tablespoon freshly ground black pepper

One 8-pound boneless tied leg roast (ask your butcher to remove the hip bone)

1. In a roasting pan, combine the tomatoes, olive oil, rosemary, garlic, salt, and pepper to make a marinade. Put the lamb in the pan and coat with marinade. Place rosemary sprigs under the butcher's twine. Cover the entire pan with plastic wrap and marinate the lamb overnight in the refrigerator. Turn it over a few times.

2. The next day, remove the lamb from the refrigerator and let it stand about 1 hour, to come to room temperature. Preheat the oven to 300° F. Pull the rosemary out from the twine and put it under the meat. Generously salt the surface of the lamb right before putting it in the oven. Pour in 1 cup of water around the lamb. Roast for about 2 hours for medium-rare, or 2 1/2 for medium. The meat should be very tender and the tomatoes should be broken down into a sauce with the lamb juices. If the tomatoes look dried out, add another cup of water and mix it up.

3. Raise the heat to 425° F. and roast about 10 more minutes, or until the meat browns on top.

4. Remove and let stand 10 minutes, then slice parallel to the bone. Spoon the sauce on top.

Lentils and Cotechino Sausage

If you don't know what cotechino sausage is, you'll love it. Really, it is just a huge sausage with a sweet, intense garlic flavor. It is also incredibly tender. Make this dish on New Year's Eve, because in Italy, lentils are considered a lucky symbol of money, and cotechino is symbolic of abundance.

ACTIVE TIME ~ 30 min. TOTAL TIME ~ 3 hr. 20 min. PORTIONS ~ 6-8

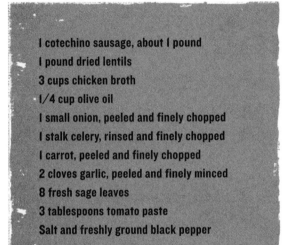

1 cotechino sausage, about 1 pound

1 pound dried lentils

3 cups chicken broth

1/4 cup olive oil

1 small onion, peeled and finely chopped

1 stalk celery, rinsed and finely chopped

1 carrot, peeled and finely chopped

2 cloves garlic, peeled and finely minced

8 fresh sage leaves

3 tablespoons tomato paste

Salt and freshly ground black pepper

1. Soak the cotechino in cold water for 2 hours. Clean the lentils well by soaking them briefly and changing the water at least once. Put them in cold water, bring to a boil, and cook until they are not quite done, about 45 minutes. Drain.

2. Wrap the cotechino in cheesecloth and pierce it with a fork several times. Boil it very slowly in the chicken broth for 50 minutes, skimming off any fat that accumulates. When the cotechino is cooked, remove it from the broth. Unwrap it from the casing and let it cool briefly.

3. In a large sauté pan, heat the olive oil and sauté the onion, celery, carrot, garlic, and sage leaves until the onion is transparent and the vegetables are limp. Add the tomato paste and blend it in with a wooden spoon. Add the lentils and 3 ladles of the broth. Season with salt and pepper. Slice the sausage and serve it on top of the vegetable and lentil mixture

Slow-Roasted Pork Shoulder

This recipe was inspired by whole roasted porchetta, truly one of the most delicious things in the world. The best I ever had was on the side of the road outside an Italian city called Arezzo. Unfortunately, many home kitchens are not designed to accommodate such a thing, but this recipe re-creates the experience pretty closely, right down to the crispy skin.

ACTIVE TIME ~ 20 min. TOTAL TIME ~ 1 Day, 7 hr. PORTIONS ~ 6

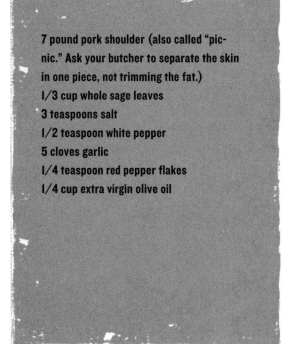

7 pound pork shoulder (also called "picnic." Ask your butcher to separate the skin in one piece, not trimming the fat.)

1/3 cup whole sage leaves

3 teaspoons salt

1/2 teaspoon white pepper

5 cloves garlic

1/4 teaspoon red pepper flakes

1/4 cup extra virgin olive oil

1. With a sharp knife, make a few shallow slashes in the fatty side of the pork. Trim about 1 tablespoon of fat from the skin and put it in the food processor with all the other ingredients, except the pork. Make a paste and rub it all over the pork.

2. Wrap the pork in plastic wrap and refrigerate overnight. Put the skin, inside-out, in the refrigerator uncovered to dry out.

3. The next day, remove the pork and the skin and preheat the oven to 300° F. When the pork gets to room temperature (about 1 hour), put it on a rack in a roasting pan and put it in the oven. Roast it for about 5 hours. Take the pan out and place the skin under the rack. Return the pan to the oven for 30 minutes.

4. Remove the pork and let it rest. Drain the excess fat from the pork into a small stockpot and set aside. Turn the oven heat up to 400° F and put the pigskin back in the pan and crisp it, which will take about 15 minutes. Remove it and slice. Slice the meat and serve with slices of the skin.

Clams Oreganata, p. 84

Pollo Sotto Mattone, p. 171

Grilled Bass, p. 152

Sfringi, p. 231

Lamb Chops Scottaditto, p. 174

Nicolina's Favorite Cheesecake, p. 233

Elena's Easter Cookies, p. 228

Elena's Biscotti, p. 230

Trippa alla Romana

When you find out what tripe is, someone invariably is there to say, "it's a delicacy." Most "delicacies" are things that sound pretty unappetizing if you've never tried them, but at some point, people were forced to eat them because they were poor and couldn't waste any possibly edible part of an animal. Well, let's all take a moment to thank the peasants of the world for braving the unknown. Tripe can be wonderful. Here it is in a simple, slightly hot tomato sauce as is typical in Rome.

ACTIVE TIME ~ 30 min. TOTAL TIME ~ 2 hr. 30 min. PORTIONS ~ 4

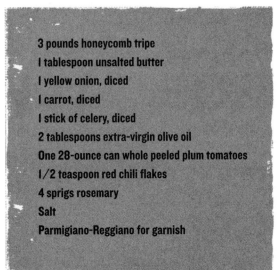

3 pounds honeycomb tripe

I tablespoon unsalted butter

I yellow onion, diced

I carrot, diced

I stick of celery, diced

2 tablespoons extra-virgin olive oil

One 28-ounce can whole peeled plum tomatoes

I/2 teaspoon red chili flakes

4 sprigs rosemary

Salt

Parmigiano-Reggiano for garnish

1. Bring a large pot of water to a boil. Add a big pinch of salt when it starts to simmer. Clean the tripe thoroughly in cold water and slice it in 1/2-inch-wide pieces. Boil the tripe for 1 hour.

2. Sauté the onion, carrot, and celery in the butter in a large skillet over medium-low heat for the last 15 minutes the tripe is boiling.

3. Drain the tripe well in a colander and raise the heat under the skillet to medium-high. Add the olive oil and then the tripe to the skillet. When the tripe browns slightly, which will take about 5 minutes, add the tomatoes with their juice, the chili flakes, and rosemary.

4. Bring this to a boil and then lower it to a simmer, taste for salt, and adjust. Lower the heat and simmer for about 1 hour, or until the tripe is tender. Serve with Parmigiano-Reggiano.

Rabbit Cacciatora

Cacciatora means "hunter-style." That definition was more apt in my early childhood, when I ate rabbit at my grandmother's house, than it is now that I buy it from my butcher. Then, the rabbit was freshly slaughtered, not exactly hunted but raised on her property. I know a lot of people out there are squeamish about rabbit. If you are one of them, I urge you to try it. If you must, replace the rabbit with chicken or veal because this sauce is just too tasty to overlook.

ACTIVE TIME ~ 20 min. TOTAL TIME ~ 1 hr. 30 min. PORTIONS ~ 4

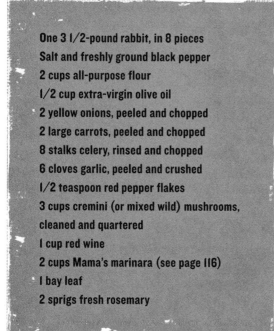

One 3 1/2-pound rabbit, in 8 pieces
Salt and freshly ground black pepper
2 cups all-purpose flour
1/2 cup extra-virgin olive oil
2 yellow onions, peeled and chopped
2 large carrots, peeled and chopped
8 stalks celery, rinsed and chopped
6 cloves garlic, peeled and crushed
1/2 teaspoon red pepper flakes
3 cups cremini (or mixed wild) mushrooms, cleaned and quartered
1 cup red wine
2 cups Mama's marinara (see page 116)
1 bay leaf
2 sprigs fresh rosemary

1. Season the rabbit pieces with a sprinkle each of salt and pepper and dredge them in the flour. In a large skillet, over high heat, brown the rabbit on all sides in the olive oil. Remove the rabbit from the pan and set aside.

2. Turn on the flame and add the onions, carrots, celery, garlic, and red pepper flakes. Sweat until the vegetables are soft, about 15 minutes. Turn the heat to medium and add the mushrooms. Cook 5 minutes. Add the red wine and reduce by about half. (Let the wine simmer and it will thicken fairly quickly.) This is deglazing. As the wine cooks off, scrape the bottom of the pan with the edge of a wooden spoon to release the tasty bits stuck to the bottom.

3. Return the rabbit, skin-up, to the pan, and cover it with the marinara; add the herbs. Bring the sauce to a boil, reduce the heat to a simmer, cover, and braise until the meat is fork-tender, about 45 minutes. Taste periodically to adjust the seasoning. Serve hot.

Roasted Rabbit and Potatoes

This is a special dish that will most often be made when an Italian relative is visiting. By the way, that's generally a good time to stop by, as there is a feast every night for up to a month. Roasting the potatoes around the meat is a staple. The potatoes pick up a lot of flavor.

ACTIVE TIME ~ 10 min. TOTAL TIME ~ 50 min. PORTIONS ~ 4

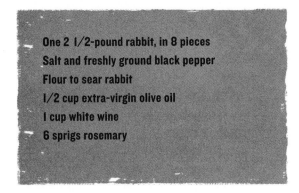

One 2 1/2-pound rabbit, in 8 pieces
Salt and freshly ground black pepper
Flour to sear rabbit
1/2 cup extra-virgin olive oil
1 cup white wine
6 sprigs rosemary

8 cubanelle peppers, whole
4 Idaho potatoes, quartered, peeled
8 cloves garlic, peeled and smashed
1 Spanish onion, peeled and sliced
4 tablespoons extra-virgin olive oil

1. Preheat the oven to 350° F.

2. Season the rabbit pieces with a sprinkle each of salt and pepper and dredge them in the flour. In a large skillet, over high heat, brown the rabbit on all sides in the olive oil. Remove the rabbit from the pan and set aside.

3. Put all the ingredients in a roasting pan and roast 30 minutes. Remove rabbit. Return potatoes to the oven if necessary, 10–15 minutes.

Porterhouse and Potatoes alla Mama

We were all a little anemic as kids, so we ate as much red meat as my parents could afford. Often on a Saturday night, my mom would buy a gigantic porterhouse steak, big enough for the whole family, sprinkle it with every dry spice she could think of, broil it, and place it in front of my father. He would then slice pieces off and pass them out to the family. I guess that sounds funny now. I think it was a slightly macho thing, but we all ate plenty. Now we eat much more.

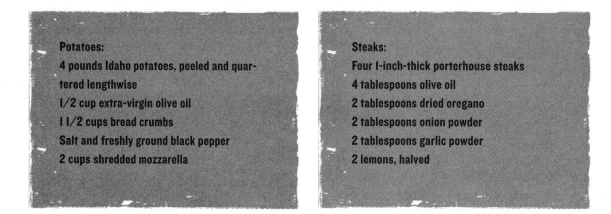

ACTIVE TIME ~ 15 min.   TOTAL TIME ~ 1 hr. 15 min.   PORTIONS ~ 4-6

Potatoes:
4 pounds Idaho potatoes, peeled and quartered lengthwise
1/2 cup extra-virgin olive oil
1 1/2 cups bread crumbs
Salt and freshly ground black pepper
2 cups shredded mozzarella

Steaks:
Four 1-inch-thick porterhouse steaks
4 tablespoons olive oil
2 tablespoons dried oregano
2 tablespoons onion powder
2 tablespoons garlic powder
2 lemons, halved

1. Preheat the oven to 350° F.

2. In a small bowl, mix together the bread crumbs, 1/2 cup olive oil, and a pinch of salt and pepper.

3. Toss the potatoes with the olive oil, bread crumbs, and salt. They should have a thin coating. Spread them on a baking sheet and roast for 1 hour, or until golden brown. Sprinkle the mozzarella over the top and roast 5 more minutes.

4. Preheat the broiler. Put the steaks in the broiler pan and coat them on both sides with the olive oil, oregano, onion powder, and garlic powder. Season the steaks generously with salt and pepper.

5. Broil the steaks for 5 minutes, then turn and broil the second side for an additional 3-5 minutes. Remove and let rest while you finish the potatoes.

6. Turn the oven down to 400° F and put the potatoes back in. Bake them until the cheese is melted and beginning to brown, about 3 minutes. Squeeze half a lemon on each steak and serve with the potatoes.

Dry-Aged Rib-Eye alle Bracce

Steak doesn't need much when it's really good. If you can find it, buy dry-aged steak, preferably aged more than three weeks (you can order it through the Internet). After you taste it, plain old steak from the butcher, even a good butcher, will seem bland. Grilling meat over white embers is the best possible method, especially using grill baskets, which allow you to control contact with the fire. *Alle bracce* means "in the branches."

ACTIVE TIME ~ 10 min. TOTAL TIME ~ 50 min. PORTIONS ~ 4

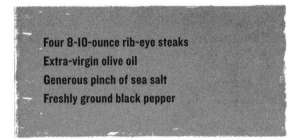

Four 8-10-ounce rib-eye steaks
Extra-virgin olive oil
Generous pinch of sea salt
Freshly ground black pepper

1. Build a hot fire with natural wood chips in your barbeque. When the chips have become glowing embers, your fire is ready.

2. Rub the steaks with olive oil, salt, and pepper, on both sides. Place them in the grill basket and cook for about 7 minutes on each side for medium rare.

Mama's Barbequed Flank Steak

Here, Mama does pure U.S.A. and does it well. Flank steak is excellent for grilling. Remember to slice it against the grain.

ACTIVE TIME ~ 10 min. TOTAL TIME ~ 1 hr. 10 min. PORTIONS ~ 4

2 tablespoons spicy mustard
1 tablespoon honey
3/4 cup barbeque sauce (your favorite brand)
2 pounds flank steak

1. In a small bowl, combine the mustard, honey, and barbeque sauce and slather it over the meat. Marinate the steak for 1 hour.

2. On a grill, cook the steaks for about 4 minutes per side for medium rare.

Braised Short Ribs Pizzaiola

Pizzaiola means "in the style of the pizza maker." It is believed that this dish was invented by the wives of pizza makers, using leftovers from the day's work. This is a variation on the more common steak pizzaiola, which is cooked only briefly in the sauce. Braising the short ribs promotes more of a penetrated flavor of the sauce in the meat.

ACTIVE TIME ~ 25 min.   TOTAL TIME ~ 4 hr. 30 min.   PORTIONS ~ 4

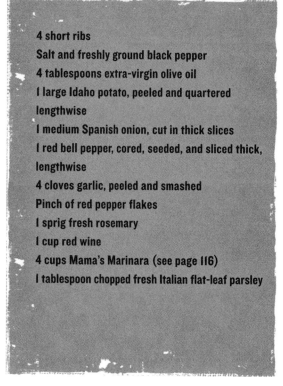

4 short ribs
Salt and freshly ground black pepper
4 tablespoons extra-virgin olive oil
1 large Idaho potato, peeled and quartered lengthwise
1 medium Spanish onion, cut in thick slices
1 red bell pepper, cored, seeded, and sliced thick, lengthwise
4 cloves garlic, peeled and smashed
Pinch of red pepper flakes
1 sprig fresh rosemary
1 cup red wine
4 cups Mama's Marinara (see page 116)
1 tablespoon chopped fresh Italian flat-leaf parsley

1. Preheat the oven to 375° F.

2. Season the short ribs generously on all sides with salt and pepper. In a very hot cast-iron skillet, heat the olive oil and sear the meat on all sides. Remove the ribs from the pan and turn off the heat.

3. In the same pan, sauté the onions, pepper, and garlic. After a few minutes, when the onions and peppers have turned slightly brown and softened, turn the heat to low. Add a pinch of salt and a pinch of red pepper flakes and rosemary. Deglaze the pan with the red wine, heating until the wine cooks down by half.

4. Add the marinara sauce and return the ribs to the pan. Pour in enough water to cover the meat (about 6 cups). Bring to a simmer on the stovetop, then transfer it to the oven and cook for 3 1/2-4 hours. Add the potatoes after 3 hours. The meat should be quite tender. Sprinkle with the parsley and serve hot.

Roast Beef

This is a Christmas dish very similar to the filet mignon on the next page. And yes, we have them both on Christmas.

ACTIVE TIME ~ 10 min. TOTAL TIME ~ 5 hr. 45 min. PORTIONS ~ 4

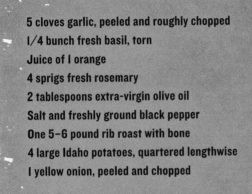

5 cloves garlic, peeled and roughly chopped

1/4 bunch fresh basil, torn

Juice of 1 orange

4 sprigs fresh rosemary

2 tablespoons extra-virgin olive oil

Salt and freshly ground black pepper

One 5–6 pound rib roast with bone

4 large Idaho potatoes, quartered lengthwise

1 yellow onion, peeled and chopped

1. In a large bowl, make a marinade of the garlic, basil, orange juice, rosemary, and olive oil, and marinate the beef in the refrigerator for 3-4 hours, turning every 30 minutes. Remove and let come to room temperature, 1 hour. Scrape off any solids and salt the beef generously on all sides.

2. Preheat the oven to 350° F.

3. Place the beef in a roasting pan and roast for 15 minutes. Add potatoes. Roast 30 minutes. Raise the heat 450° F. Roast 10 minutes more.

Filet Mignon

This is a very posh Christmas dish from my family. After the seven fishes on Christmas Eve, everyone's ready for some meat, and things are kept a lot more straightforward after the elaborate feast of the night before. That's not to say that we don't have another enormous feast; it's just that the dishes themselves require less preparation.

ACTIVE TIME ~ 10 min.   TOTAL TIME ~ 2 hr. 10 min.   PORTIONS ~ 4-6

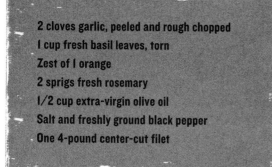

2 cloves garlic, peeled and rough chopped

I cup fresh basil leaves, torn

Zest of I orange

2 sprigs fresh rosemary

1/2 cup extra-virgin olive oil

Salt and freshly ground black pepper

One 4-pound center-cut filet

1. Make a marinade paste in the food processor. Rub all over the beef and marinate for 1 hour, at room temperature.

2. Preheat the oven to 450° F.

3. Roast the filet on a rack for 15 minutes, or until the top gets browned a little. Turn the heat down to 350° F and roast for another 45 minutes. Let it stand for about 10 minutes before slicing.

C

ontorni are Italian side dishes, traditionally referring only to vegetables. In Italy, there are no sides of spaghetti. Like most home cooks in America, Italians — at home as well as in restaurants — do not eat composed dishes like we are used to in American restaurants, where the main item, meat or fish, usually comes predictably flanked by one starch and one vegetable. In my house when I was growing up, there was protein like meat, fish, or eggs, with one or two (or nine) contorni.

Contorni

Soft Polenta

Soft polenta is, to me, one of the ultimate comfort foods. To my relatives, it's the ultimate poverty food. Though it has become a regular component of dishes at the finest restaurants, ironically, my uncle Silvio refuses to touch it because it reminds him of being poor in Italy. The following version has the addition of Parmigiano-Reggiano, which is unconventional but seems like the most natural step. Leave it out if you think your mother would gasp. Or put it in for just that reason.

ACTIVE TIME ~ 15 min. TOTAL TIME ~ 20 min. PORTIONS ~ 4

- 5 cups water
- 1 cup fine polenta
- 1/2 cup grated Parmigiano-Reggiano
- Salt and freshly ground black pepper
- 2 teaspoons extra-virgin olive oil

1. Bring the water to a boil in a large saucepan. Slowly pour in the polenta, stirring constantly with a whisk. Cook for about 10 minutes. Turn the heat down and add the Parmigiano-Reggiano, salt and pepper to taste, and the olive oil. Serve hot.

Cousin Angela's Escarole with White Beans and Pig Skin Braciola

In my family, my cousin Angela is the culinary star of my generation. You might think it's me, but in terms of mastering the most traditional methods and instincts, it's Angela. This is a good example of her faithfulness to the motherland. When she handed over this recipe, she told me, "This is *really* Italian. This is hometown food!"

ACTIVE TIME ~ 25 min. TOTAL TIME ~ 1 hr. 15 min. PORTIONS ~ 4

- 2 cloves garlic, peeled and chopped
- 1 tablespoon extra-virgin olive oil
- 2 cups chicken broth
- 2 bunches escarole, cleaned, trimmed, chopped
- Two 4-inch-square pieces of pig skin (from your butcher)
- 2 teaspoons salt
- 4 cranks freshly ground black pepper in a mill
- 2 tablespoons chopped fresh Italian flat-leaf parsley
- 2 tablespoons grated Parmigiano-Reggiano
- 1 tablespoon seasoned bread crumbs
- 1/2 pound dried cannellini beans, soaked overnight

1. In a stockpot, sauté the garlic in the olive oil over medium heat until light golden brown and tender, 5 minutes.

2. Pour in the chicken stock and 4 cups of water and bring to a boil. Blanch the escarole and remove it with a slotted spoon.

3. Meanwhile, make the braciola: lay the pieces of pig skin out flat. Sprinkle them with the salt, pepper, parsley, Parmigiano-Reggiano, and bread crumbs. Roll them up and tie each with butcher's twine or spear with tooth-picks to keep them closed. Set them aside.

4. Add the pig skin to the chicken stock and simmer for 45 minutes, or until the skin is tender. Add the escarole and cook for 15 minutes. Then add the beans and cook for 5 more minutes. Remove everything from the pot with a slotted spoon and serve.

Ditalini Mascarpone

While developing the menu for Rocco's, my cooks and I wondered what would happen if we treated ditalini like risotto. The answer? The starches in pasta can be coaxed out to make a creamy coating just like the starches in rice. And it takes less time. When we added mascarpone, we created the Italian macaroni and cheese!

ACTIVE TIME ~ 15 min. TOTAL TIME ~ 20 min. PORTIONS ~ 4

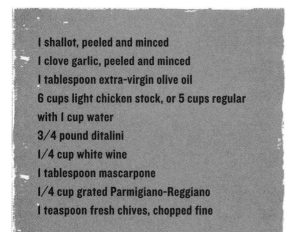

I shallot, peeled and minced

I clove garlic, peeled and minced

I tablespoon extra-virgin olive oil

6 cups light chicken stock, or 5 cups regular with I cup water

3/4 pound ditalini

1/4 cup white wine

I tablespoon mascarpone

1/4 cup grated Parmigiano-Reggiano

I teaspoon fresh chives, chopped fine

1. Sweat the shallot and garlic in a saucepot with the olive oil, about 6 minutes. Meanwhile, bring the stock to a boil in a small pot and turn off the heat.

2. Add the pasta to the garlic and shallot. Stir to coat, 2 minutes. Add the wine and stir until it is absorbed. Add 1 ladle of stock at a time, stirring constantly and adding another ladle when the liquid has been absorbed. Repeat until the pasta is cooked through but is not mushy.

3. Remove from the heat and mix in the mascarpone and Parmigiano. Top with the chives before serving.

Sautéed Spinach

This is my go-to vegetable side-dish. It's as simple as they get. The only trick is to cook it *very* briefly.

ACTIVE TIME ~ 5 min. TOTAL TIME ~ 10 min. PORTIONS ~ 4

2 tablespoons extra-virgin olive oil

1 clove garlic, peeled and smashed

3 bunches spinach

1. In a wide skillet, sauté the garlic in exta-virgin olive oil over medium-low heat, stirring occasionally, until the garlic is tender and only slightly golden brown, about 8 minutes. Add the spinach. It will all fit as the spinach wilts. Do not cover. The spinach will cook very quickly. Remove as soon as it has wilted and turned dark green.

Mama's Roasted Potatoes

This dish evolved out of roasting potatoes with meat, as is done with the Porterhouse and Potatoes alla Mama (see page 184). Aside from tasting great, this is an easy way to cook for a lot of people at once. Eventually, my mom improved upon those potatoes by adding something that makes everything better: cheese.

ACTIVE TIME ~ 10 min. TOTAL TIME ~ 1 hr. 15 min. PORTIONS ~ 4

4 large Idaho potatoes, peeled and quartered lengthwise.

1 tablespoon extra-virgin olive oil

1/4 cup bread crumbs

1/2 teaspoon salt

2 cups grated mozzarella

1. Preheat the oven to 350° F.

2. Toss the potatoes with the olive oil, bread crumbs, and salt. They should have a thin coating. Spread them on a baking sheet and roast for 1 hour, or until golden brown. Sprinkle the mozzarella over the top and roast 5 more minutes.

Braised Fennel

Fennel was often eaten raw before or after meals in my house when I was growing up, but braised fennel makes a great side dish with fish or meat. It goes especially well with sausage.

ACTIVE TIME ~ 15 min.   TOTAL TIME ~ 1 hr. 20 min.   PORTIONS ~ 4

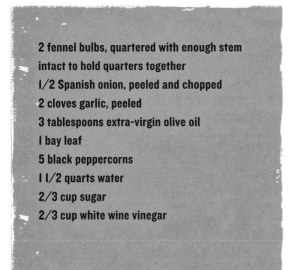

2 fennel bulbs, quartered with enough stem
intact to hold quarters together

1/2 Spanish onion, peeled and chopped

2 cloves garlic, peeled

3 tablespoons extra-virgin olive oil

1 bay leaf

5 black peppercorns

1 1/2 quarts water

2/3 cup sugar

2/3 cup white wine vinegar

1. Trim the tops of the fennel bulbs off, leaving just the round, white bottoms. Set them aside.

2. Use the tops to make a fennel broth: sweat the onion and garlic in a stockpot with 2 tablespoons of the olive oil, the bay leaf, fennel tops (chop them in big pieces if necessary to fit in pot), and peppercorns. Add the water, sugar, and vinegar and bring the mixture to a boil. Lower the heat to a simmer and cook uncovered for about 30 minutes. Strain through a fine mesh sieve or, better, a cheesecloth, reserving the broth and discarding the solids.

3. Preheat the oven to 350° F.

4. Heat the remaining 1 tablespoon of olive oil in a deep ovenproof pot over medium-high heat. Caramelize the fennel in the skillet on all sides. Add the stock to the pot and put it in the oven for about 30 minutes, or until the fennel is very tender.

Stuffed Roasted Peppers

This dish is an Italian-American classic. It alone could be a perfect lunch at room temperature. We loved stuffed things, you may have noticed. It's funny, considering that my relatives cannot understand Thanksgiving stuffing, but this they have down.

ACTIVE TIME ~ 30 min. TOTAL TIME ~ 1 hr. 35 min. PORTIONS ~ 4

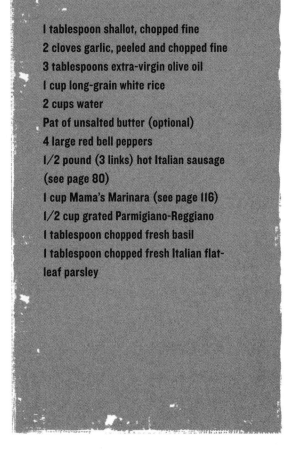

I tablespoon shallot, chopped fine

2 cloves garlic, peeled and chopped fine

3 tablespoons extra-virgin olive oil

I cup long-grain white rice

2 cups water

Pat of unsalted butter (optional)

4 large red bell peppers

1/2 pound (3 links) hot Italian sausage (see page 80)

I cup Mama's Marinara (see page 116)

1/2 cup grated Parmigiano-Reggiano

I tablespoon chopped fresh basil

I tablespoon chopped fresh Italian flat-leaf parsley

1. Preheat the oven to 375° F.

2. In a small pot, sweat the shallot and garlic in 2 tablespoons olive oil over low heat until they become tender, about 10 minutes. Add the rice and stir to coat in the oil. Add the water to the rice and, if you want, a pat of butter. Bring to a low simmer and cover for 20 minutes.

3. Meanwhile, roast the peppers by placing each one on a burner of your stove, over medium heat, until they soften. Turn with tongs before the skin blackens, as it will not be peeled. Remove the peppers and let them cool on a rack. Then trim the tops and scoop out the seeds, being careful not to tear the sides.

4. Remove the sausages from their casings and brown them in a hot cast-iron skillet with 1 tablespoon extra-virgin olive oil, breaking them into bite-size pieces with a spoon in the pan.

5. When the rice is cooked, combine it in a bowl with the sausage, marinara (it's not necessary to heat the sauce since it will be baked), Parmigiano-Reggiano, basil, and parsley.

6. Using a spoon and holding the peppers, stuff them with the rice mixture. Again, be careful not to tear the skins. Place them in a medium casserole and drizzle with extra-virgin olive oil. Bake the peppers for 30 minutes, covered. Remove the cover and bake 15 more minutes.

Farinata

When my mother was a young girl, flour was scarce and her mother, my grandmother, would grind different grains or beans into flour to make bread. I am not sure whether she used chickpeas, or *ceci*, in that way, but no doubt this dish was invented out of such scarcity.

ACTIVE TIME ~ 20 min. **TOTAL TIME** ~ 3 hr. 40 min. **PORTIONS** ~ 10

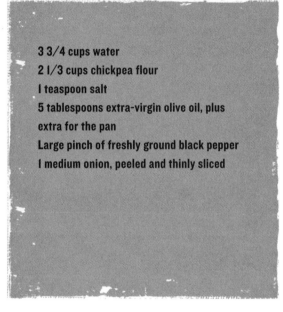

3 3/4 cups water

2 1/3 cups chickpea flour

I teaspoon salt

5 tablespoons extra-virgin olive oil, plus extra for the pan

Large pinch of freshly ground black pepper

I medium onion, peeled and thinly sliced

1. Preheat the oven to 400° F.

2. Put the water in a large bowl. Slowly whisk in the chickpea flour. Add the salt. Let the mixture stand at room temperature for 3 hours, or even better, overnight. Remove the foam from the top.

3. Grease a 16-by-12-inch baking pan with olive oil. Once greased, add another 2 tablespoons of olive oil. Add the chickpea mixture. Use a fork to combine the olive oil and chickpea mixture. Sprinkle generously with the pepper.

4. Heat the remaining 3 tablespoons of olive oil in a medium nonstick pan over medium heat. Add the onion and cook for about 10 minutes.

5. Top the farinata with the onion slices and bake for 20 to 25 minutes. Remove the pan from the oven and let it cool for about 10 minutes before cutting and serving.

Giambotta di Nicolina

This dish could be made with endless combinations of vegetables. *Giambotta* just means "hodgepodge." My mom's version has always been a favorite of mine, but it's a good method to keep in mind when you have some seemingly random ingredients in your kitchen and you're hungry.

ACTIVE TIME ~ 15 min. TOTAL TIME ~ 20 min. PORTIONS ~ 4

2 tablespoons extra-virgin olive oil
3 cloves garlic, peeled and smashed
1/4 Spanish onion, peeled and sliced thick
I red bell pepper, cored, seeded, and sliced thick

I green bell pepper, cored, seeded, and sliced thick
6 cremini mushrooms, trimmed and cleaned
1/4 yellow squash, seeded and chopped

1. In a skillet, sauté the garlic and onion over medium heat in the olive oil. Meanwhile, cut all the vegetables into big chunks. When the garlic is tender and slightly browned, add the vegetables and stir them around until they are tender, about 10 minutes.

Verdure, Room Temperature

At about 99 percent of the meals I ever ate at home or at either of my uncles' houses, at least one green vegetable was served in this style. It is similar to sautéed greens, but the vegetables are less cooked, more vibrant, and eaten at room temperature. This is common in Italy, where many restaurants have an antipasto bar.

ACTIVE TIME ~ 15 min. TOTAL TIME ~ 35 min. PORTIONS ~ 4

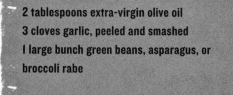

2 tablespoons extra-virgin olive oil
3 cloves garlic, peeled and smashed
I large bunch green beans, asparagus, or broccoli rabe

1. Over medium heat, in a skillet, heat the olive oil and cook the garlic until it is very light golden brown, 5-6 minutes.

2. Meanwhile, bring a large pot of water to a boil with plenty of salt in it. Blanch the green vegetable of your choice for about 3 minutes, then drain.

3. Prepare an ice bath and shock the vegetable. Drain in a colander and wrap in paper towels to dry well. When the garlic is brown, turn the heat off, add the vegetable to the skillet, toss to coat with the oil. Serve the vegetable at room temperature.

Stolen Dandelions

When I was very young, our Greek neighbors used to steal the dandelions that grew wild in front of our house. I always wondered what they could possibly want with the weeds. Now I know that dandelions are a delicious bitter green.

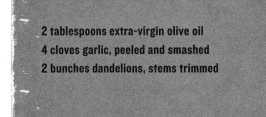

ACTIVE TIME ~ 10 min. TOTAL TIME ~ 30 min. PORTIONS ~ 4

2 tablespoons extra-virgin olive oil

4 cloves garlic, peeled and smashed

2 bunches dandelions, stems trimmed

1. Bring a large pot of salty water to a boil. In a skillet, heat the olive oil and slowly brown the garlic in it, 5-6 minutes. When the water comes to a boil, drop the dandelions in and blanch them for about 2 minutes. Then remove them from the water with a slotted spoon and shock them in an ice bath. Shake and pat them dry. Put the dandelions in the skillet with the garlic and sauté for about 7-8 minutes over low heat, until the dandelions are warm.

String Beans Patata

Italians are starch-crazed maniacs. They want to cook every vegetable with potatoes. Is it because it will make them fat? Because it feels so good in your mouth? Because it's cheap? I don't know, but here is one good reason. This is one of the ultimate summer dishes.

ACTIVE TIME ~ 10 min. TOTAL TIME ~ 35 min. PORTIONS ~ 4

4 large Idaho potatoes, peeled and quartered

2 bunches string beans, trimmed

2 tablespoons extra-virgin olive oil

1/2 tablespoon red wine vinegar

2 teaspoons fresh oregano

2 cloves garlic, peeled and minced

2 teaspoons red pepper flakes

Salt

1. Boil the potatoes in heavily salted water for about 8 minutes. Then add the string beans to the water and boil another 3-4 minutes. Drain both and pat them dry.

2. In a large bowl, combine the olive oil, vinegar, oregano, garlic, and red pepper flakes. Toss the potatoes and string beans in the dressing and let stand at least 10 minutes to reach room temperature and absorb the dressing. Taste and season with salt, and serve.

alads, especially green salads,
were always served at the end of the meal in my
family. Because I'm used to it, roughage seems
like the perfect end to a meal. Even after a big
meal when I am too full, eating salad seems like a
good idea. But on a summer day, it's all I need.

Insalata

Chopped Salad

Every proper pizzeria has a version of this salad. Feel free to add your own touches, like diced salami, anchovies, or pepperoncini.

ACTIVE TIME ~ 10 min. TOTAL TIME ~ 10 min. PORTIONS ~ 4

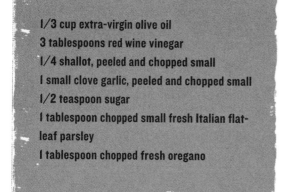

1/3 cup extra-virgin olive oil

3 tablespoons red wine vinegar

1/4 shallot, peeled and chopped small

1 small clove garlic, peeled and chopped small

1/2 teaspoon sugar

1 tablespoon chopped small fresh Italian flat-leaf parsley

1 tablespoon chopped fresh oregano

1 teaspoon chopped fresh basil

1 head romaine lettuce, chopped

1/4 head iceberg lettuce, chopped

1 head radicchio, chopped

1 large cucumber, seeds removed, chopped

1/2 red onion, chopped

1/4 pound provolone, diced

Salt and freshly ground black pepper

1. In a small bowl, whisk together the olive oil, vinegar, shallot, garlic, sugar, and herbs. Drizzle over the lettuces, cucumbers, onions, and cheese. Season with salt and pepper to taste.

Tomato and Onion Salad

This is an Italian-American standby but also an old-school New York favorite. It is about the only thing on the menu at the famous Peter Luger steak house in Brooklyn, aside from steak. As uneventful as it sounds, when tomatoes are good, this is a great salad in the middle of a hot day or next to a hot steak. When tomatoes are out of season, don't even try it. It wouldn't be right.

ACTIVE TIME ~ 5 min. TOTAL TIME ~ 5 min. PORTIONS ~ 4

3 large tomatoes, preferably heirloom if they are in season, sliced thick

1/2 large red onion, halved and sliced thin

2 tablespoons extra-virgin olive oil

Sea salt and freshly ground black pepper

2 teaspoons aged balsamic vinegar

1. Toss the tomato and onion together in a bowl with the olive oil and salt and pepper to taste. Arrange on a serving plate and drizzle with the balsamic vinegar.

Caesar Salad

Shockingly, Caesar salad was created in Mexico, but it was the Italians who added the anchovy, so my pride is intact. Bad Caesar salads seem to have invaded the country. Beware of poseurs. The recipe below is the real deal, which does mean there is raw egg in the dressing. Although the chances are extremely rare, be aware that it is possible to be poisoned by salmonella when eating raw eggs. To me, it's worth the risk, but be your own judge, and let your guests know as well.

ACTIVE TIME ~ 20 min. TOTAL TIME ~ 40 min. PORTIONS ~ 4

2 marinated anchovies, chopped fine

1 egg yolk

1 teaspoon garlic, chopped

1 teaspoon shallots, chopped

Juice of 1 lemon

1 dash Worcestershire sauce

1 teaspoon grainy mustard

1 teaspoon Dijon mustard

1/2 teaspoon freshly ground black pepper

1/4 cup extra-virgin olive oil

1/2 cup canola oil

1/4 cup grated Parmigiano-Reggiano, plus more shaved for garnish

1 tablespoon chopped fresh Italian flat-leaf parsley

1/4 teaspoon salt and 1/4 cayenne pepper

3-4 thick slices white bread (preferably a few days old, slightly dry)

4 romaine hearts, chopped

1. Preheat the oven to 375° F for the croutons.

2. Whisk together the anchovies, egg yolks, garlic, shallots, lemon juice, Worcestershire, and mustards. Season with black pepper. Combine the oils in a measuring cup and begin whisking the oil into the egg mixture slowly to form an emulsion. Whisk until all of the oil has been incorporated. Stir in the Parmigiano and parsley and season to taste with salt and cayenne pepper.

3. To make croutons, cut the bread into 1-2 inch cubes and spread them out on a baking sheet. Drizzle generously with extra-virgin olive oil and sprinkle with plenty of salt. Bake for 10-15 minutes, or until they are just barely browned and crunchy. Let them cool before tossing in the salad, so they don't wilt your lettuce.

4. Chop the romaine in thick pieces, trimming the very tops. Toss the salad, adding the dressing gradually. Depending on your taste, you may have more dressing than you need.

Caprese Salad

What can be said about this perfect, patriotic-looking salad? Like a lot of Italian food, it is only as good as its ingredients. There is nothing to hide behind here, so get the freshest mozzarella and make this only during high tomato season! Make sure the mozzarella is room temperature before serving. If it's cold, the flavor will not be as palpable.

ACTIVE TIME ~ 10 min. TOTAL TIME ~ 10 min. PORTIONS ~ 4

4 tomatoes

8 ounces fresh mozzarella

10 fresh basil leaves

Extra-virgin olive oil

Aged balsamic vinegar

Salt

1. Slice the tomatoes into 1/2-inch-thick slices starting at the bottom to avoid the stem. Slice the mozzarella into 1/2-inch-thick slices and layer it with the tomato and whole basil leaves, alternating among the 3 ingredients.

2. Drizzle the salad with extra-virgin olive oil. (This is the time to use the good stuff. It makes a big difference.) Sprinkle with a few drops of aged balsamic vinegar and salt to taste, and serve.

When I was eleven years old, I got my first job ever, and the first of three consecutive summer jobs at pizzerias in Queens. In those three years, nothing was more torturous than the idle dream of actually being the one to make the pizza. In Italy and, as far as I was concerned, in Queens, no one is cooler than the pizzaiolo. That's why the owner was always the only person who got to do it. With the following recipes, we can all have our day as the pizzaiolo. There is only one bread recipe in this book because there is only one all-encompassing bread recipe in my family.

Pizza and Bread

Basic Pizza Dough

The pizza is your canvas! You don't need to mess with perfection, but, well why not do it anyway? You can make a great pizza at home with anything and everything you like and have around. You think it's going to fall through the grill, but it seizes up and becomes the crispiest pizza ever. You'll feel like David Copperfield. Have fun.

ACTIVE TIME ~ 20 min. TOTAL TIME ~ 1 hr. 10 min. PORTIONS ~ 4

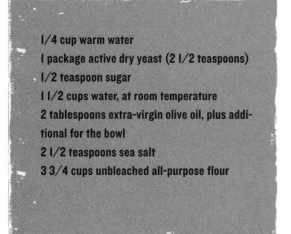

1/4 cup warm water

1 package active dry yeast (2 1/2 teaspoons)

1/2 teaspoon sugar

1 1/2 cups water, at room temperature

2 tablespoons extra-virgin olive oil, plus additional for the bowl

2 1/2 teaspoons sea salt

3 3/4 cups unbleached all-purpose flour

1. Pour the 1/4 cup of warm water into a large bowl. Add the yeast and sugar, and stir to combine. Let stand about 10 minutes, or until the yeast has dissolved and the mixture is foamy.

2. Add the 1 1/2 cups room temperature water, 2 tablespoons olive oil, and the salt to the yeast mixture. Stir in 3 1/2 cups of the flour, 1/2 cup at a time, until a slightly sticky dough forms. Knead the dough on a floured surface until it is smooth and elastic, adding more flour by tablespoonfuls if the dough is too sticky, about 10 minutes.

3. Brush a large bowl with olive oil and place the dough in it. Brush the top of the dough with more olive oil. Cover the bowl with plastic wrap and let the dough rise in a warm spot until it has doubled in volume, about 45 minutes.

Grilled Pizza Dough

Grilled pizza is a great thing. It is an incredibly social endeavor, as your friends and family can all hang around the grill, taking turns customizing their pizzas. Also, the dough gets a slight charred or smoky flavor from the wood. The dough can be held for 1 day in the refrigerator. Let sit 1 hour at room temperature before grilling.

ACTIVE TIME ~ 15 min. TOTAL TIME ~ 1 hr. PORTIONS ~ 4

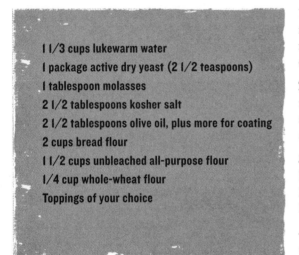

1 1/3 cups lukewarm water

1 package active dry yeast (2 1/2 teaspoons)

1 tablespoon molasses

2 1/2 tablespoons kosher salt

2 1/2 tablespoons olive oil, plus more for coating

2 cups bread flour

1 1/2 cups unbleached all-purpose flour

1/4 cup whole-wheat flour

Toppings of your choice

1. In a large bowl, combine the water, yeast, and molasses, and stir gently to mix. Set aside for about 5 minutes, until bubbly and foamy. Add the salt and olive oil, and stir to mix.

2. In a separate bowl, whisk together the flours. Add the flour to the yeast mixture, and stir with a wooden spoon until a dough forms and pulls away from the sides of the bowl.

3. Divide the dough into 6 equal pieces. Roll them into balls and place them on an oiled baking sheet. Brush the balls with olive oil and cover the pan with plastic wrap. Let the dough rise in a warm place for about 20 minutes.

4. Preheat a grill with coals on one half and bricks on the other (so that there is a hot and cool side). Assemble all of your topping ingredients on a big platter.

5. When the grill is ready, oil a second baking sheet and flatten 1 ball of dough into a 10- to 12-inch piece about 1/8 of an inch thick. A perfect circle is less crucial than even thickness.

6. Carefully stretch the dough onto the hot side of the grill and cook until the dough puffs on top, crisps on the bottom, and grill marks appear, 1-2 minutes.

7. Flip the dough onto the cool side of the grill and brush the cooked side with olive oil. Quickly and sparingly assemble the toppings on the dough.

Grilled Pizza Rustica

If you need inspiration for your grilled pizza dough, this should get you going.

ACTIVE TIME ~ 15 min. TOTAL TIME ~ 1 hr. PORTIONS ~ 4

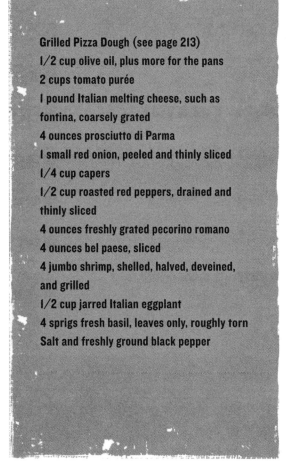

Grilled Pizza Dough (see page 213)
1/2 cup olive oil, plus more for the pans
2 cups tomato purée
1 pound Italian melting cheese, such as fontina, coarsely grated
4 ounces prosciutto di Parma
1 small red onion, peeled and thinly sliced
1/4 cup capers
1/2 cup roasted red peppers, drained and thinly sliced
4 ounces freshly grated pecorino romano
4 ounces bel paese, sliced
4 jumbo shrimp, shelled, halved, deveined, and grilled
1/2 cup jarred Italian eggplant
4 sprigs fresh basil, leaves only, roughly torn
Salt and freshly ground black pepper

1. Preheat a grill with coals on one half and bricks on the other (so that there is a hot and a cool side). Assemble all of your topping ingredients on a big platter.

2. Lightly oil a sheet pan and roll and stretch 1 ball of dough until it is approximately 12 inches in length and 8 inches across. It is not necessary to make a perfect circle, but the dough should be an even thickness of 1/8 inch. Carefully stretch the dough onto the hot side of the grill and cook until the dough puffs on top, crisps on the bottom, and grill marks appear, 1-2 minutes.

3. Flip the dough onto the cool side of the grill and brush the cooked side with olive oil. Quickly and sparingly assemble the toppings of your choice, such as tomato purée, fontina, prosciutto di Parma, red onion, capers, and red peppers, or tomato purée, pecorino romano, bel paese, grilled jumbo shrimp, and jarred Italian eggplant, onto the dough. Garnish with torn basil leaves. Feel free to improvise the toppings and come up with your own.

4. Once the pizza has been dressed, season it with salt and pepper to taste, drag it over to the hot side of the grill, and cook until the ingredients are heated through. (If the pizza browns too quickly, pull it to the cool side and cover the grill to finish cooking.) Using a wide spatula or two pairs of tongs, carefully lift the pizza onto a cutting board and slice it into 6 or 8 pieces. Serve right away. Repeat with the remaining dough.

Pizza alla Napoletana

In Naples, the birthplace of pizza, I met with the professor of pizza from Naples University (really), who told me the story of Queen Margherita's visit to Naples in 1889. Rafaelle Esposito created the patriotically colored pizza in the queen's honor and named it after her. Below is a variation on the original, but in keeping with the flag.

ACTIVE TIME ~ 25 min. TOTAL TIME ~ 1 hr. 30 min. PORTIONS ~ 4

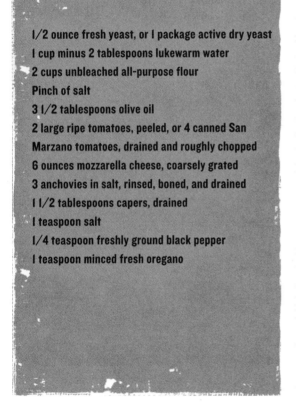

1/2 ounce fresh yeast, or 1 package active dry yeast

1 cup minus 2 tablespoons lukewarm water

2 cups unbleached all-purpose flour

Pinch of salt

3 1/2 tablespoons olive oil

2 large ripe tomatoes, peeled, or 4 canned San Marzano tomatoes, drained and roughly chopped

6 ounces mozzarella cheese, coarsely grated

3 anchovies in salt, rinsed, boned, and drained

1 1/2 tablespoons capers, drained

1 teaspoon salt

1/4 teaspoon freshly ground black pepper

1 teaspoon minced fresh oregano

1. Preheat the oven to 450° F.

2. Dissolve the yeast in the water. Pour the flour into a mound on the counter. Add the dissolved yeast, salt, and 1 tablespoon of the olive oil to the center of the flour. Work the flour into the liquid from outside with a fork until it resembles a dough. Work in the rest of the flour by hand, leaving 1 tablespoon of flour unincorporated. Place the dough in a large bowl. Sprinkle it with the leftover flour. Cover the bowl with a dish towel. Let the dough rest for about 1 hour at room temperature, until it has doubled in size.

3. Pass the tomatoes through a food mill, using the smallest holes, into a small bowl. Set aside.

4. When the dough is ready, place a sheet of heavy tinfoil on a pizza board. Oil it with 1 tablespoon of the olive oil. Spread the dough on the foil, using your fingertips, to about 16 inches by 14 inches. Spread on the puréed tomatoes. Sprinkle on the mozzarella cheese. Distribute the anchovies and capers evenly. Add the salt, pepper, and oregano. Drizzle on the remaining 1 1/2 tablespoons of olive oil.

5. Bake on middle shelf of the oven for 35 minutes, or until crisp. Remove, slice, and serve.

Torta Rustica

Make this for your family or friends. They will hail the master of deliciousness. It's a pie oozing with melted cheese, salami, and tomatoes. It is a cousin in the pizza family—it just has a top, basically.

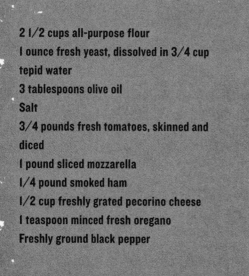

2 1/2 cups all-purpose flour

1 ounce fresh yeast, dissolved in 3/4 cup tepid water

3 tablespoons olive oil

Salt

3/4 pounds fresh tomatoes, skinned and diced

1 pound sliced mozzarella

1/4 pound smoked ham

1/2 cup freshly grated pecorino cheese

1 teaspoon minced fresh oregano

Freshly ground black pepper

1. Mound the flour on a work surface and make a well in the center. Pour the dissolved yeast, olive oil, and a pinch of salt into the center of the well. Gently mix in the flour with a fork. The dough should be smooth and pliable. (Add a little warm water if the dough is too dry.) Roll the dough into a ball and put in a floured bowl. Cover the bowl with a cloth, and put it in a warm place for about 1 hour.

2. Preheat the oven to 400° F.

3. Divide the dough into 2 pieces and roll out 1 of the pastry balls into a 9-inch circle. Lay the circle on a greased baking pan. Spread the tomatoes, mozzarella, ham, and pecorino over the dough. Sprinkle with the oregano and salt and pepper to taste. Roll out the other ball, lay it over the toppings, and fold the top and bottom layers of the dough together around the edges. Cut 3 small holes in the top of the pie to allow steam to escape. Bake in the oven for 20 minutes, or until the crust is brown and cooked through and the cheese has melted.

Everyday Bread

This is the bread I ate every day growing up. It is simple and goes well with any meal, or, for my mom at least, is a meal in itself with a little olive oil. Feel free to adjust the ratio of white to wheat flour. It could be made with 100% one or the other, but I find this version most versatile. My aunt Elena uses fresh yeast and even warms the water on the stove instead of using warm tap water. These details do make a difference in taste and texture, but you will be very happy with the results of dry yeast and tap-warm water, too.

ACTIVE TIME ~ 30 min.   **TOTAL TIME** ~ 1 hr. 30 min.   **PORTIONS** ~ one loaf, about 12 slices

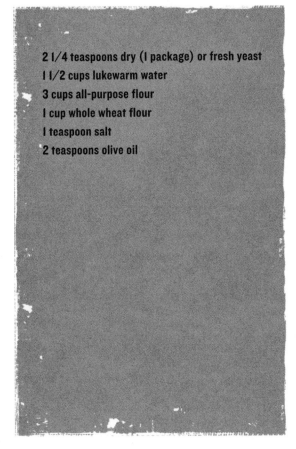

2 1/4 teaspoons dry (1 package) or fresh yeast

1 1/2 cups lukewarm water

3 cups all-purpose flour

1 cup whole wheat flour

1 teaspoon salt

2 teaspoons olive oil

1. In a small bowl, dissolve the yeast in lukewarm water. Let it sit until bubbles form on the surface.

2. Combine the flours and salt and make a mound on your work surface. Create a well in the center with your hands. Gradually pour the water/yeast mixture into the well. Using your fingers, incorporate the dry ingredients into the wet, pressing and kneading the dough until it comes together enough to handle and shape. Continue to knead the dough until it begins to form a smooth ball. Add a dash of water if necessary after 7 or 8 minutes; the dough should not be dry or brittle. Drizzle some olive oil onto your work surface and knead the dough vigorously for about 4 minutes, or until it is soft, pliable, and smooth. Shape the dough into a ball and place it in a deep bowl. Cover the bowl with a few dish towels and let it rest in a warm place for one hour, or until it is doubled in size.

3. Preheat the oven to 400° F.

4. Shape the dough into a torpedo-shaped (or round) loaf and place it on a baking sheet. Slash the loaf in three places with a very sharp knife, cover with a kitchen towel and allow to rise until nearly doubled. Place in the oven and bake until it is deep golden brown in color and produces a hollow sound when tapped on the underside, about 45 minutes. Cool on a rack.

Sandwiches were a huge part of my life growing up; there is no more perfect lunch for a kid, or an adult for that matter. Unlike traditional American deli sandwiches, mine were very often heated up, either in the oven, as are the heros on the following pages, or in a pan and pressed down (panini). In Italy, like in Cuban restaurants in New York, this is done in a press, which, by the way, is one of the best tools I can think of for a dorm room or bachelor pad. You can easily mimic the effect of the press, though, by weighting down the panino with a heavy skillet. The result is golden, crispy bread, melted cheese, and the happy marriage of all the flavors mushed together inside.

Panini and Heros

Water Buffalo Mozzarella Croque Monsieur Panini

OK, so I'm crossing the line to the French sandwich (*croquer* means "to crunch"). But these flavors are all-Italy.

ACTIVE TIME ~ 20 min. TOTAL TIME ~ 35 min. PORTIONS ~ 6

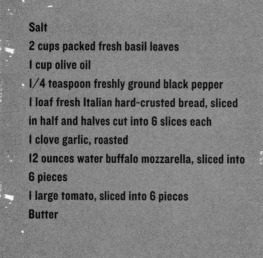

Salt

2 cups packed fresh basil leaves

I cup olive oil

1/4 teaspoon freshly ground black pepper

I loaf fresh Italian hard-crusted bread, sliced in half and halves cut into 6 slices each

I clove garlic, roasted

12 ounces water buffalo mozzarella, sliced into 6 pieces

I large tomato, sliced into 6 pieces

Butter

1. Bring 4 quarts of water to boil in a stockpot and add 3 tablespoons of salt. Set up an ice bath. Blanch the basil for 2 minutes in boiling water, then transfer it immediately to the ice bath. Cool the basil for 2 minutes, drain, then squeeze any excess water from it.

2. In a blender, combine the basil with the olive oil. Strain this mixture through a coffee filter. Season with 1 teaspoon of salt and the pepper. Rub the inside of the bread with the roasted garlic. Layer the bread with mozzarella and tomato slices. Drizzle the basil oil over the tomato slices. Heat a large cast-iron pan over a medium-high flame until very hot. Butter the outside of the sandwiches on both sides to taste. Place 3 sandwiches at a time in the heated pan and press them down with another cast-iron pan. Cook until the sandwich bottoms are brown. Turn over and brown the other side. Repeat with the remaining sandwiches, and serve hot.

Baked Sausage and Nutella Panini

This may sound insane, and maybe it just exposes me as some kind of depraved Nutella addict, but I created this dish out of the need to eat Nutella constantly. I couldn't justify Nutella and banana sandwiches for dinner, but if I got a little protein in there, I thought it just might work. I picked sausage because I love salty stuff with chocolate. Don't knock it till you try it.

ACTIVE TIME ~ 5 min. TOTAL TIME ~ 35 min. PORTIONS ~ 4

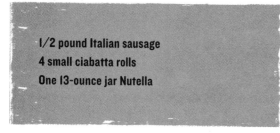

1/2 pound Italian sausage
4 small ciabatta rolls
One 13-ounce jar Nutella

1. Preheat the oven to 450° F.

2. In a large sauté pan over medium-high heat, cook the sausages until all sides are brown. Slice them lengthwise. Slice the rolls lengthwise and spread the bottoms with Nutella. Place the sausages over the Nutella. Bake the sandwiches in the oven until the bread is lightly toasted.

Eggplant and Taleggio Panini

Taleggio is a little, well, stinky, but in the greatest way.

ACTIVE TIME ~ 10 min. TOTAL TIME ~ 25 min. PORTIONS ~ 4

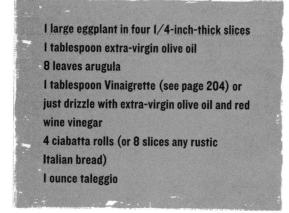

I large eggplant in four 1/4-inch-thick slices
I tablespoon extra-virgin olive oil
8 leaves arugula
I tablespoon Vinaigrette (see page 204) or just drizzle with extra-virgin olive oil and red wine vinegar
4 ciabatta rolls (or 8 slices any rustic Italian bread)
I ounce taleggio

1. Preheat the broiler for 15 minutes.

2. Thinly slice the eggplant lengthwise. Brush the slices with the olive oil and broil them or cook briefly in a grill pan. Toss the eggplant in a medium bowl with the arugula and vinaigrette. Lay 2 slices of eggplant on each roll, with 2 leaves of arugula. Add a few slices of taleggio to each sandwich, and grill them in a press or in a cast-iron skillet weighted down with another cast-iron skillet, until golden brown on both sides.

Prosciutto and Mozzarella Panini

What can I say—the world's perfect sandwich.

ACTIVE TIME ~ 15 min. TOTAL TIME ~ 15 min. PORTIONS ~ 4

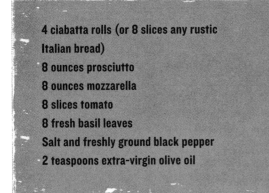

4 ciabatta rolls (or 8 slices any rustic Italian bread)

8 ounces prosciutto

8 ounces mozzarella

8 slices tomato

8 fresh basil leaves

Salt and freshly ground black pepper

2 teaspoons extra-virgin olive oil

1. On each roll, layer about 2 slices of prosciutto and mozzarella. Add 2 slices of tomato and 2 basil leaves. Sprinkle with salt and pepper, and drizzle with the olive oil. Grill each sandwich in a press or in a hot cast-iron skillet weighted down with another heavy skillet, until golden brown on both sides.

Meatball Heros

One of the best parts of having a mom who makes amazing meatballs is having the leftovers on heros. And a bonus is that you can make great ones in the toaster oven.

ACTIVE TIME ~ 15 min. TOTAL TIME ~ 25 min. PORTIONS ~ 4

4 sub rolls

4 cups Mama's Marinara (see Page 116)

8 fresh basil leaves

12 Mama's Meatballs (see page 78), cut in half

3 tablespoons grated Parmigiano-Reggiano

8 thin slices mozzarella

1. Preheat the broiler for 15 minutes.

2. Slice each roll in half and lay them flat. Spoon a few tablespoons of marinara on both sides of the bread. Next, tear 2 basil leaves and place the pieces on both sides of the bread. Put 6 meatball halves on each sandwich, leaving them open-face. Top with the Parmigiano-Reggiano and mozzarella. Place the sandwiches in the broiler to melt the cheese, about 5 minutes. Fold each sandwich together, if you can. Serve the sandwiches with extra marinara.

Chicken Parmigiana Heros

Of course, if you make chicken parm (see page 165), you can cut a piece out for a sandwich, but you don't need an excuse if you really crave the hero.

ACTIVE TIME ~ 25 min.   TOTAL TIME ~ 35 min.   PORTIONS ~ 4

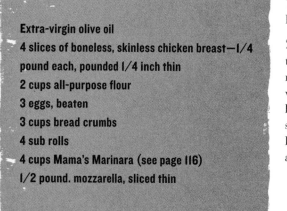

Extra-virgin olive oil

4 slices of boneless, skinless chicken breast—1/4 pound each, pounded 1/4 inch thin

2 cups all-purpose flour

3 eggs, beaten

3 cups bread crumbs

4 sub rolls

4 cups Mama's Marinara (see page 116)

1/2 pound. mozzarella, sliced thin

1. Heat the olive oil in a heavy-bottomed sauté pan. Preheat the broiler.

2. Dredge the chicken in the flour, then in the egg, and then in the bread crumbs. Fry the chicken for about 2 minutes. Place the chicken on a cookie rack or a plate with paper towels to absorb excess oil. Slice each roll in half and lay them flat. Spoon some marinara onto both sides. Lay the chicken down. Top with the mozzarella. Place the sandwiches in the broiler to melt the cheese, about 5 minutes. Serve the heros with the extra marinara.

Like any kid, I liked sweet things when I was young, but for me they were almost exclusively linked with holidays and other special occasions. My mother was never as interested in baking as she was in cooking savory dishes. We often ate fruit at the end of the meal, or simply finished with a green salad or sliced raw fennel. But my aunt Elena loves both cooking and baking and is famous for her cookies especially. Then there were the pastries from Italian-American bakeries and that friends brought on certain holidays. We never saw those being prepared, and they were a special treat partly for that reason.

Dolce

Zia Elena's Easter Cookies

My aunt Elena is the main baker in the family. If you saw her house during Easter time, you'd have to assume she had snuck to the bakery and was trying to trick us into thinking she had done it all herself. But she had, and in addition to old traditions like this one, she keeps inventing more. These colorfully sprinkled cookies are still strictly linked to Easter in my mind.

ACTIVE TIME ~ 25 min.   TOTAL TIME ~ 45 min.   PORTIONS ~ 6

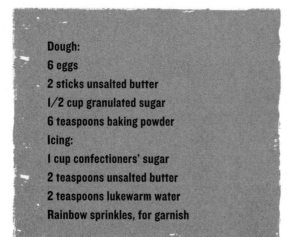

Dough:
6 eggs
2 sticks unsalted butter
1/2 cup granulated sugar
6 teaspoons baking powder
Icing:
I cup confectioners' sugar
2 teaspoons unsalted butter
2 teaspoons lukewarm water
Rainbow sprinkles, for garnish

1. Preheat the oven to 400° F. Grease a baking sheet.

2. In a large bowl, combine the eggs, butter, granulated sugar, and baking powder. The dough should be thick and dense but not sticky.

3. Pull off a small handful of dough and roll it into a long, thin log. Make a tight, flat spiral with the log on the baking sheet. Repeat to use all the dough.

4. Bake the cookies for 20 minutes. Let cool on a rack. Combine the confectioners' sugar, butter, and water in a small bowl to make a thin paste. Then glaze the logs with the icing, using a pastry brush. Top with a generous amount of rainbow sprinkles.

Elena's Cream Puffs

My sister, Maria, still eats these until her stomach hurts. This is probably the most luxurious dessert on Long Island. The puffs have a thin, crisp shell, and the inside is airy, silky, and sweet.

ACTIVE TIME ~ 20 min. TOTAL TIME ~ 40 min. PORTIONS ~ 4

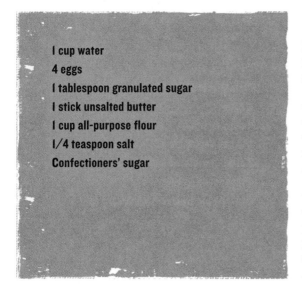

I cup water

4 eggs

I tablespoon granulated sugar

I stick unsalted butter

I cup all-purpose flour

I/4 teaspoon salt

Confectioners' sugar

1. Preheat the oven to 400° F.

2. Bring the water to a boil in a small pot over medium-low heat. Meanwhile, beat the eggs and sugar together in a bowl until they are creamy and light.

3. When the water comes to a boil, add the butter and stir until it melts. Then add the flour and turn the heat off. Stir until the mixture comes together and away from the sides of the pot. Pour the mixture into a bowl and set aside to cool for about 3 minutes.

4. When the butter/flour mixture cools, it should be sticky and thick. Add the eggs/sugar mixture and mix just to combine. Scoop 1-tablespoon balls onto a prepared baking sheet and bake for 20 minutes. They should have a very light golden color. Let them cool and sprinkle with confectioner's sugar if you want.

Biscotti

When Maria decided her cookie repertoire ought to include biscotti, she didn't mess around. These are the best biscotti I've ever had. Initially they were a Christmas tradition, but they became a regular item in Maria's house because no one could stand to wait for the holidays to dip them in coffee or grappa. They are too good. Make the chocolate chip dough, roll it into a log, and slice off the cookies, or make that dough and the plain biscotti dough and roll them together for fancy-looking, delicious biscotti.

ACTIVE TIME ~ 45 min. TOTAL TIME ~ 1 hr, 30 min. PORTIONS ~ 6

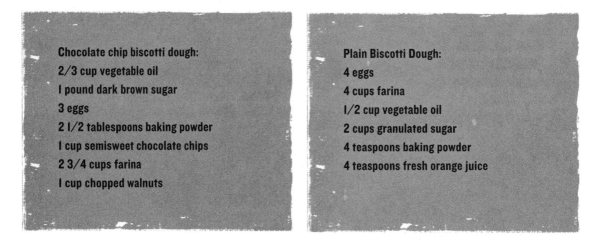

Chocolate chip biscotti dough:
2/3 cup vegetable oil
I pound dark brown sugar
3 eggs
2 1/2 tablespoons baking powder
I cup semisweet chocolate chips
2 3/4 cups farina
I cup chopped walnuts

Plain Biscotti Dough:
4 eggs
4 cups farina
1/2 cup vegetable oil
2 cups granulated sugar
4 teaspoons baking powder
4 teaspoons fresh orange juice

1. Preheat the oven to 400° F.

2. Make chocolate chip dough: Mix oil and sugar together. Add all other ingredients and mix until even. Roll flat, about 1/2 inch thick.

3. Make plain dough: Combine all of the ingredients to make a smooth dough. Roll the dough flat.

4. Roll out the chocolate chip dough and place it on top of the plain dough. Trim the edges and roll the stacked dough tightly together. Slice the log into 1/2-inch-thick cookies, and twist each cookie at the edges.

5. Place the cookies on an ungreased baking sheet and bake for about 50 minutes.

Sfringi

Sfringi may not roll off the tongue, but your friends will be screaming for them once they try these deep-fried cookies. Here is my mother's recipe. She and my aunt Elena make them into a variety of shapes. My favorite are bow ties.

ACTIVE TIME ~ 30 min. TOTAL TIME ~ 45 min. PORTIONS ~ 6

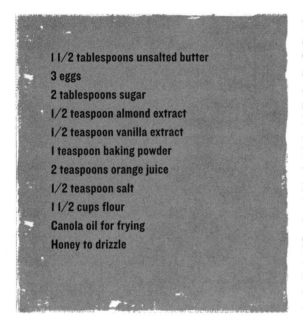

1 1/2 tablespoons unsalted butter

3 eggs

2 tablespoons sugar

1/2 teaspoon almond extract

1/2 teaspoon vanilla extract

1 teaspoon baking powder

2 teaspoons orange juice

1/2 teaspoon salt

1 1/2 cups flour

Canola oil for frying

Honey to drizzle

1. Melt the butter over the stove or in the microwave and set aside so it's not too hot when you need it. Combine the eggs and sugar in a bowl. Add the almond and vanilla extracts and stir to combine. Then gradually whisk in the butter. Add the baking powder and salt and mix to combine. Add the flour gradually and knead until the dough comes together. Transfer the dough to a work surface with a little flour on it and knead it until it's smooth and only a little sticky, about 7-8 minutes. Roll the dough into a ball and wrap it in plastic. Let it rest for 10-15 minutes. (You could make the dough several hours before frying it if necessary. Just be sure to wrap it tight.)

2. Unwrap the dough and cut it into 5 or 6 small pieces. Put each one through a pasta machine several times, starting on the biggest setting (#1) and moving down each time to the second smallest (#5). If you do not have a pasta machine, roll the dough as thin as you can get it.

3. Lay the sheets of dough flat on a work surface. Cut each one lengthwise so they are about 2-2 1/2 inches wide. The length doesn't matter. With a ridged roller-cutter, slice the sheet across on a diagonal, about 1 inch wide. Separate the pieces and then make a short slit with the roller cutter in the middle of each slice, as if to cut it in half lengthwise, but not reaching either end. Pick up one piece and insert one end into the slit in the middle and pull it through gently. Lay the sfringi out flat on a little flour.

4. Fill a deep pot 1/3 up with canola oil and heat it until a drop of water sizzles violently as soon as it is dropped onto the oil. Fry the sfringi, a few at a time, until they are very light golden brown. They should have lots of puffy air pockets. Remove them with a slotted spoon and place them on a cookie rack or paper towels for a minute, to drain any excess oil. Drizzle honey over them and serve hot.

Cannoli Napoletane

I love candied orange peel in cannoli. The bitterness is balanced out by the creamy filling. On the exposed openings of the tube, you can dip one side of the cannoli in chocolate chips and the other in orange.

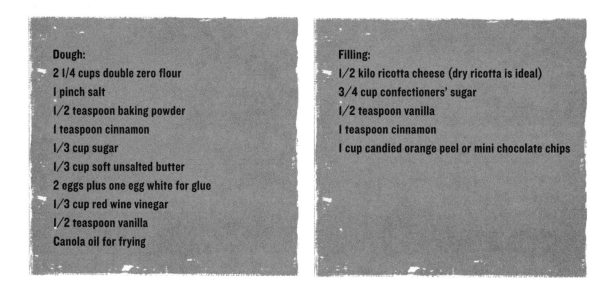

ACTIVE TIME ~ 45 min.   TOTAL TIME ~ 50 min.   PORTIONS ~ 6

Dough:
2 1/4 cups double zero flour
I pinch salt
1/2 teaspoon baking powder
I teaspoon cinnamon
1/3 cup sugar
1/3 cup soft unsalted butter
2 eggs plus one egg white for glue
1/3 cup red wine vinegar
1/2 teaspoon vanilla
Canola oil for frying

Filling:
1/2 kilo ricotta cheese (dry ricotta is ideal)
3/4 cup confectioners' sugar
1/2 teaspoon vanilla
I teaspoon cinnamon
I cup candied orange peel or mini chocolate chips

1. In an electric mixer, combine all the dry ingredients and butter till you have a grainy paste. Add the whole eggs and red wine vinegar just till incorporated. Cover with plastic and refrigerate overnight.

2. Flatten the dough out and pass it through a pasta machine once at setting size 4, or roll it out about 1/8 inch thick and cut it into triangles about 4 inches long on one side and about 3 inches on the other 2 sides.

3. Heat enough canola oil to fill a tall pot about 1/3 up.

4. Meanwhile, form the triangles into tubes by wrapping them around something round (a small rolling pin would work). The hollow inside should be about 1-1 1/2 inches wide. Place the long side of the triangle along the length of your dowel, and wrap the opposite point around to meet the center of that long side. Lightly beat the egg white with a fork and use it to glue the edges together, pressing lightly to make it stick. Carefully slide the cannoli shells off the dowel and fry each until light golden brown. Remove them to a rack or paper towels to drain the excess oil and cool in shape.

5. While the cannoli shells cool, make the filling: In an electric mixer, whip ricotta until soft. Add the sugar, then the vanilla and cinnamon. With a pastry bag with no tip, pipe the cream into the cannoli. If you do not have a pastry bag, just fill a large Ziploc bag with the filling, pushing out the air bubbles, and then cut one bottom corner off, making an opening about 1 inch wide. Dip the exposed edges in chocolate chips or candied orange peel (or anything else you can think of).

Nicolina's Favorite Cheesecake

This is my mother's favorite dessert, and I think it's pretty fitting. The reason it's so good is that the filling is half ricotta and half cream cheese. We took the best from the old and new worlds, Italy and New York, so this is the perfect hybrid Italian-American recipe, and it works. If you can find dry ricotta, it's the best choice for baking, but regular supermarket stuff is fine. If it seems very wet, suspend it in cheesecloth overnight.

ACTIVE TIME ~ 20 min. TOTAL TIME ~ 1 hr. PORTIONS ~ 8

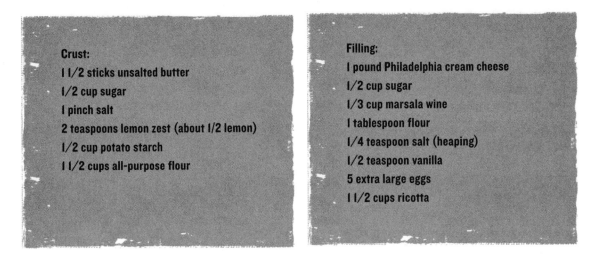

Crust:
- 1 1/2 sticks unsalted butter
- 1/2 cup sugar
- 1 pinch salt
- 2 teaspoons lemon zest (about 1/2 lemon)
- 1/2 cup potato starch
- 1 1/2 cups all-purpose flour

Filling:
- 1 pound Philadelphia cream cheese
- 1/2 cup sugar
- 1/3 cup marsala wine
- 1 tablespoon flour
- 1/4 teaspoon salt (heaping)
- 1/2 teaspoon vanilla
- 5 extra large eggs
- 1 1/2 cups ricotta

1. Cream the butter, sugar and salt. Add the lemon zest. Add the potato starch and flour. Mix to combine thoroughly. The dough should come together quickly in an electric mixer. Push it into a ball and wrap it tightly in plastic. Refrigerate for at least 30 minutes.

2. Preheat the oven to 400° F. Remove the dough to a lightly floured work surface and roll it out thin into a circle, about 14 inches in diameter. Line a 10-inch pie plate and crimp the edges. Trim any excess dough. Place a sheet of heavy-duty tin foil in the pie shell and weight it down with dried loose beans or pie weights. Bake the piecrust for 15 minutes, just until it loses its raw look and takes on a tiny bit of color, but doesn't brown. Remove the tin foil and weights and allow the crust to cool to room temperature, about 15-20 minutes. Lower the oven heat to 325° F.

3. While the piecrust is cooling, make your filling. Whip the cream cheese and sugar. Add the marsala and stir to combine. Add the flour, salt, and vanilla. Combine. Add the eggs one at a time, allowing each to be incorporated into the mixture before the next is added. Stir in the ricotta till the mixture is uniform.

4. When the piecrust has cooled, pour the filling into the pie shell and bake it for 45 minutes. The filling should be set and just slightly wobbly in the very center. The top should be golden brown.

Elena's Ricotta Grain Cake

Until Elena gave me this recipe recently, none of my cousins or I could agree on what the grain in this cake was. I remembered it as wheat berries, while others swore it was rice. Some just said, "It's grain," unable to put a name on it. It is a little earthier and less sweet than the other ricotta cheesecake I have included, and it has a pleasant orange taste that really goes well with grappa.

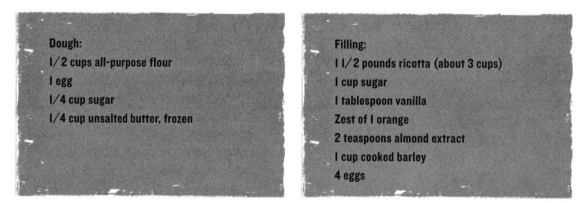

ACTIVE TIME ~ 30 min.   TOTAL TIME ~ 1 hr. 40 min.   PORTIONS ~ 12

Dough:

1/2 cups all-purpose flour

I egg

1/4 cup sugar

1/4 cup unsalted butter, frozen

Filling:

I 1/2 pounds ricotta (about 3 cups)

I cup sugar

I tablespoon vanilla

Zest of I orange

2 teaspoons almond extract

I cup cooked barley

4 eggs

1. In a food processor, combine the dry ingredients for the dough. Add the butter until it's flaky. Then add the eggs 1 at a time. Add 2-3 tablespoons ice water till it comes together. Roll it out thin and refrigerate for at least 1 hour.

2. Meanwhile, make the filling. Combine all ingredients in a large bowl and mix till smooth. Refrigerate. Preheat the oven to 100° F.

3. Roll the piecrust onto an 11-inch pie plate and push down gently. Weight down the shell with beans and bake for 15 minutes. Remove and set aside to cool for 5 minutes.

4. Pour filling into shell. Bake for 1 hour. Test the center and return to oven for 15 minutes if the center is not cooked.

Chocolate Walnut Budino

This is basically a warm chocolate pudding that no one can pass up. I developed it with my pastry chef at Rocco's, thinking we had to have chocolate, and Italians love nuts with chocolate. Walnuts are grown in Campagna, among other regions. So even though this recipe doesn't come from Italy, it is very much in the style of Italian desserts.

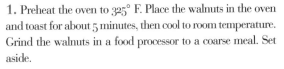

ACTIVE TIME ~ 20 min.   **TOTAL TIME** ~ 50 min.   **PORTIONS** ~ 2-3

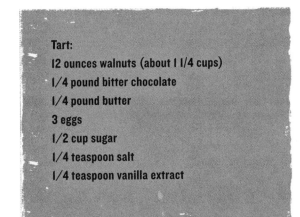

Tart:

12 ounces walnuts (about 1 1/4 cups)

1/4 pound bitter chocolate

1/4 pound butter

3 eggs

1/2 cup sugar

1/4 teaspoon salt

1/4 teaspoon vanilla extract

1. Preheat the oven to 325° F. Place the walnuts in the oven and toast for about 5 minutes, then cool to room temperature. Grind the walnuts in a food processor to a coarse meal. Set aside.

2. Melt chocolate and butter in a double boiler.

3. Whip eggs and sugar together until light in color and frothy. Add the salt and vanilla.

4. Add the ground walnuts to the egg mixture, then fold the mixture into the chocolate mixture. Pour the batter into a buttered 8-inch cake pan or ovenproof bowl of similar size. Bake for 30 minutes at 325° F.

Sauce:

1 1/4 cups whole roasted walnuts

1 1/2 cups sugar

1/4 cup flour

1/2 teaspoon salt

3 ounces butter

1 1/2 cups heavy cream

1/4 tablespoon vanilla extract

1. Combine dry ingredients in a bowl. Combine butter and cream over medium heat in a small saucepot, stirring constantly to avoid burning the bottom. Add all dry ingredients. Simmer until thick, 5 minutes.

Zeppole

The secret ingredient in these zeppole is lemon zest. It's very subtle, but it gives these fried dough balls a little kick. Make sure the oil is very hot before frying them, so they are very light and crisp. Put them in a paper bag with a heaping spoonful of confectioners' sugar, close the bag, and shake. If you do this when the zeppole are still very hot, the steam inside will make the sugar start to melt and make a glaze.

ACTIVE TIME ~ 30 min.   TOTAL TIME ~ 1 hr. 20 min.   PORTIONS ~ 4

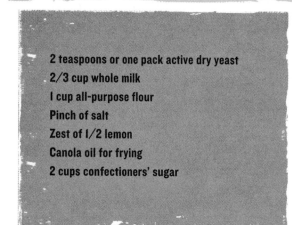

2 teaspoons or one pack active dry yeast
2/3 cup whole milk
1 cup all-purpose flour
Pinch of salt
Zest of 1/2 lemon
Canola oil for frying
2 cups confectioners' sugar

1. In a small bowl, dissolve the yeast in the milk. In a large bowl, combine this with the flour, salt, and zest into a thick, smooth batter. Let stand for about 45 minutes or until it triples. The batter will become spongy and should quadruple in volume.

2. In a heavy-bottomed stockpot, bring the canola oil to at least 350° and no hotter than 375° F. Fry the zeppole in the oil until they are very light golden brown. Remove and drain the zeppole on a paper towel briefly. Then shake the zeppole and liberal spoonfuls of confectioners' sugar in a paper bag. Eat right away.

Zabaglione

My grandmother used to make zabaglione with a fresh egg for my sister, Maria, who was anemic. The men had it in the morning with their coffee, at night with marsala, and with fruit anytime. This one has a strong marsala taste, which I love, but if you like it more mild, reduce marsala to 1/2 cup.

ACTIVE TIME ~ 20 min.   TOTAL TIME ~ 20 min.   PORTIONS ~ 4

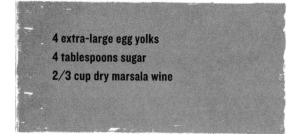

4 extra-large egg yolks
4 tablespoons sugar
2/3 cup dry marsala wine

1. In a double boiler over low heat, stir the egg yolks and sugar together, until the sugar is completely mixed into the yolks and the color lightens. Add the marsala slowly, stirring constantly. It will foam on top and gradually thicken. Do not stop whisking and do not allow it to boil! Remove the pan from the heat as soon as the zabaglione starts to coat the back of a spoon, about 15 minutes. Transfer it to a new bowl to cool, then serve.

Banana Fritta

Italians eat fruit for dessert more than anything else, so even though this dessert seems totally whimsical and un-Italian, I think it's clever. Not only does it sneak the fruit in, but it also uses the frying technique that, in my opinion, was perfected in Naples.

ACTIVE TIME ~ 15 min.   TOTAL TIME ~ 30 min.   PORTIONS ~ 4

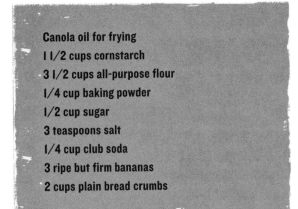

Canola oil for frying

1 1/2 cups cornstarch

3 1/2 cups all-purpose flour

1/4 cup baking powder

1/2 cup sugar

3 teaspoons salt

1/4 cup club soda

3 ripe but firm bananas

2 cups plain bread crumbs

1. Heat the canola oil in a heavy-bottomed stockpot over medium heat.

2. In a medium bowl, combine the cornstarch, flour, baking powder, sugar, and salt. Add the club soda, and mix until smooth. Put this bowl inside a larger bowl filled with ice water.

3. Cut the bananas into thirds, giving you three short columns. Dredge the bananas in the batter and then in the bread crumb, and drop them carefully in the hot oil. Remove the fritta when they turn golden brown. Serve with Vanilla Gelato (see page 242).

Peaches in Wine and 7UP

My grandmother loved to poach peaches in wine with 7UP for dessert. The men would drink it straight, but my grandmother, mother, and aunts always watered theirs down further with soda. They never got drunk.

ACTIVE TIME ~ 10 min.   TOTAL TIME ~ 35 min.   PORTIONS ~ 4

4 fresh peaches, peeled and chopped in wedges

4 cups red wine

2 cups 7UP

1. Combine all of the ingredients in a large saucepan and boil on the stovetop until reduced by almost half. The peaches should be soft.

Elena's Blueberry Cake

If you ever happen to be in West Hempstead in the late morning, drop by my aunt Elena and uncle Joe's house. This is where my grandmother lived until she died. Elena, like my grandmother, only cooks in the basement, although she renovated her "show" kitchen recently with faux marble counters and new appliances. The kitchen in the basement suits her better. My uncle Joe and his brother, Silvio, who lives two doors down, will be sitting at the table down there, watching TV, and likely eating this blueberry cake and drinking coffee. Soon you will be eating this cake, too, and when you have to go, Elena will wrap up what's left in tinfoil and give it to you.

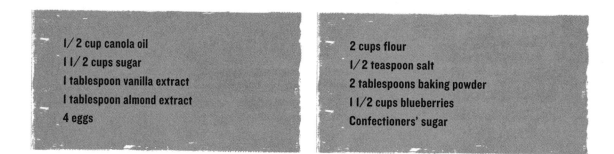

ACTIVE TIME ~ 25 min. TOTAL TIME ~ 1 hr. 15 min. PORTIONS ~ 4

1/2 cup canola oil
1 1/2 cups sugar
1 tablespoon vanilla extract
1 tablespoon almond extract
4 eggs

2 cups flour
1/2 teaspoon salt
2 tablespoons baking powder
1 1/2 cups blueberries
Confectioners' sugar

1. Preheat the oven to 350° F. Lightly grease a 9-inch cake pan.

2. With an electric mixer beat the canola oil and sugar together until you have a light, grainy paste. Add the vanilla and almond extract and mix to combine. Then add the eggs one at a time, allowing each to be fully incorporated into the batter before adding the next. Turn off the mixer as soon as the last egg has been mixed in.

3. In a separate bowl, mix the flour, salt, and baking soda together. Turn the electric mixer on a low setting and add the dry ingredient mix gradually to the batter. Stop mixing as soon as the dry ingredients are fully incorporated and you have a smooth, thick, golden batter. Pour the batter into your cake pan and shake to even the top. Place the berries on the surface of the batter, close together, pushing them in very slightly, covering the entire surface.

4. Bake for 45 minutes and test by inserting a cake tester or sharp knife into the center. It will come out clean when the cake is done. The top of the cake should be golden brown. It may take up to an hour. If after 45 minutes the top is brown but the inside is still uncooked, lower the heat to 325° F and test every ten minutes. Remove the cake and let it cool for about ten minutes. Sprinkle generously with confectioners' sugar and serve hot or at room temperature.

People usually say that gelato is Italian ice cream, which is true, in a sense. Do not take that to mean that *gelato* is simply the Italian word for "ice cream." The two differ in that gelato contains much less cream fat, a lot less air, and usually more egg yolks, so it's lighter in a way, but has a denser consistency because it doesn't have nearly as much air whipped into it. It also lacks the filmy, greasy aftertaste ice cream sometimes has from the fat. It has an even creamier, silkier mouthfeel. It is also more intensely flavored than ice cream, which always, at its base, tastes like cream. Going to the gelateria in Italy is an occasion in itself, like going to the movies is here. There's nothing better, and you can find gelato in most cities in the States, if you look hard enough. If you are truly dedicated, buy a gelato machine, which will make that difference in the amount of air whipped in. If you have an ice cream machine, these recipes will work great but will be a little fluffier than gelato should be.

Gelato

Nocciola Gelato

In Italy, hazelnut ice cream is as basic as chocolate and vanilla are here. Italians love hazelnuts and consider them a sweet nut. They use them in many desserts for their sweetness and their aromatic quality. If you love Nutella, maybe you don't even realize it, but you love hazelnuts.

ACTIVE TIME ~ 20 min. TOTAL TIME ~ 55 min. PORTIONS ~ I quart

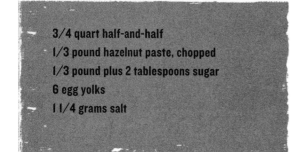

3/4 quart half-and-half
1/3 pound hazelnut paste, chopped
1/3 pound plus 2 tablespoons sugar
6 egg yolks
1 1/4 grams salt

1. In a medium saucepan, bring the half-and-half to a boil with the hazelnut paste and sugar. Temper the egg yolks in carefully. Let the mixture come back to a boil. Remove the pan from the heat and strain the mixture through a chinoise or cheesecloth into a medium bowl. Set that bowl inside a larger bowl of ice water. Put through machine as manufacturer instructs.

Vanilla Gelato

They may be hard to find, but using real vanilla beans will make all the difference in your ice cream and gelato. Good vanilla ice cream always has little specks of the black seeds.

ACTIVE TIME ~ 20 min. TOTAL TIME ~ 55 min. PORTIONS ~ I quart

3/4 quart half-and-half
I vanilla bean, cut in half lengthwise
1/3 pound plus 2 tablespoons sugar
6 egg yolks
1 1/4 grams salt

1. In a medium saucepan, bring the half-and-half to a boil with the vanilla bean and sugar. Temper the egg yolks in carefully. Let the mixture come back to a boil. Remove the pan from the heat and strain the mixture through a chinoise or cheesecloth into a medium bowl. Set that bowl inside a larger bowl of ice water. Put through machine as manufacturer instructs.

Chocolate Rum Gelato

You should, of course, leave out the rum if you're making a gelato sundae for a minor, but if it's all grown-ups, this is very elegant. The rum and chocolate are simply a perfect match.

ACTIVE TIME ~ 30 min.   TOTAL TIME ~ 1 hr.   PORTIONS ~ 2 quarts

I quart whole milk

2 cups heavy cream

1/4 cup corn syrup

2/3 cup dry milk

1 1/3 cups sugar

1 1/2 sheets gelatin

3 cups half-and-half

I vanilla bean

3/4 cup sugar

1 1/2 pounds bittersweet chocolate

6 egg yolks

1/4 cup rum, or to taste

1. Put the milk, cream, corn syrup, dry milk, and sugar in a sauce pot over medium-high heat and bring this to a boil. Remove the pan from the fire and let the mixture cool for about 5 minutes. Add the gelatin.

2. In a medium saucepan, bring the half-and-half to a boil with the vanilla beans and sugar. Turn off the heat and melt in the chocolate. Temper the egg yolks in carefully. Let the mixture come back to a boil. Remove the pan from the heat and strain the mixture through a chinoise or cheesecloth into a medium bowl. Set that bowl inside a larger bowl of ice water. Add the rum by taste, and run through machine according to manufacturer's instructions.

These sorbettos have a light, airy texture, not the icy shards of the past. There is nothing more refreshing I can think of than fruity frozen desserts. They remind me of summers in Queens when I worked the Italian ices cart outside the pizzeria where I held the important position of "the summer kid." The flavors were bubble gum, red, and lemon-flavored; I was obsessed with the bubble gum, which was blue, so I would dig it all out of the "rainbow" bin and eat it before it sold, leaving me with a blue face and a very upset stomach. Well, you have to start somewhere. These are a step or two up from those days.

Sorbetto

Raspberry Sorbetto

ACTIVE TIME ~ 10 min.   TOTAL TIME ~ 45 min.   PORTIONS ~ 4

4 cups water
4 cups simple syrup
8 cups frozen raspberry purée
Juice of 1 lemon

1. Add the water and syrup to the purée. Put through ice cream machine according to the manufacturer's instructions.

Blueberry Sorbetto

ACTIVE TIME ~ 10 min.   TOTAL TIME ~ 45 min.   PORTIONS ~ 4

4 cups fresh orange juice
4 cups simple syrup
8 cups frozen blueberry purée
Juice of 1 lemon

1. Add the orange juice and syrup to the purée. Strain the purée. Put through ice cream machine according to the manufacturer's instructions.

Apple Sorbetto

ACTIVE TIME ~ 10 min.   TOTAL TIME ~ 45 min.   PORTIONS ~ 4

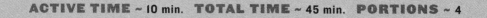

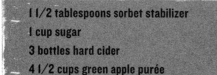

1 1/2 tablespoons sorbet stabilizer
1 cup sugar
3 bottles hard cider
4 1/2 cups green apple purée
Juice of 1 lime

1. Mix the stabilizer with the sugar. Mix the cider with the purée. Combine all and put through machine according to the manufacturer's instructions.

The Italian-American Pantry

When my parents came to this country, many of these ingredients were impossible to find here. Today, almost everything on the list below can be found fairly easily; if not the authentic, imported version, then something produced in the United States that's pretty close. If you live somewhere where there is no Little Italy but there is a Greek neighborhood, or a Mediterranean or Middle Eastern population, you may find some of these ingredients in their markets, especially things like good (and often less expensive) olive oil, anchovies, pickled peppers, spices, dried beans, and harder-to-find fishes and meat, like porgy, rabbit, and baby lamb.

Whether you're a devoted Italian food expert or an occasional cook, keep the basics on hand to use in just about any kind of dish — an invention of your own or any recipe in this book. The meat, fish, and fresh vegetables you will have to buy when you are ready to use them, but once you get them home, you'll have everything you need.

In restaurants, we call the area where the raw food is prepared the *garde manger*, which means "guard" or "protect" the food. This is the idea of the pantry, too. In my grandmother's house, there is still a room called the cantina just off the basement kitchen. It is dark, with uninsulated brick walls, and therefore perfect for storage. My aunt Elena and uncle Joe keep their canned tomatoes, pickled peppers, and oil in there still, and their homemade sausages and wine in the garage. This list applies to the food you store in your kitchen, generally. Of course, things like meat and fish are kept in the fridge, but all other basics should ideally be kept in a cool, dark place. Take note in the advice below what should be kept in the coolest spots if you, like most Americans, don't have a cantina like my aunt's. But if you have an unfinished basement, garage, or attic, take advantage of it, especially if you stock up on pantry items. If you live in a house or apartment that has a 1950s-style cold box in the kitchen, don't think it outdated; I wish I had one for salumi, cheese, eggs, and olive oil.

In my mother's cooking, and in Italian-American cooking as a whole, the essential trinity of ingredients is extra-virgin olive oil, Parmigiano-Reggiano, and tomatoes. Do not attempt to cook without them!

Extra-Virgin Olive Oil

There are a few things you should know about extra-virgin olive oil. First, the younger the better. Unlike fine wine, it does not age well. Olive oil is pressed in November and the bottled product has a vintage. Look for the most recent vintage you can find. Unfortunately, you will often find that the vintage is not even noted on the label, which probably means it's a very old olive oil.

If you can find a good young one, buy a small bottle and keep it in the refrigerator. Do not use this for cooking. Use it as a garnish for finished dishes. This oil may seem expensive, and for a small amount, but you will use it sparingly on bread, drizzled over fish, or a few drops into a bowl of soup (see Caprese Salad, page 207). Keeping olive oil in a cool place is the key to retaining its taste, and will also cause a slight thickening or viscosity that will let you drizzle with precision and make the oil act like a sauce. The fanciest chefs keep their extra-virgin olive oil in an ice bucket next to them while they work! It is also ideal to keep olive oil in a dark place, just like wine. This is when a basement cantina comes in handy. If you have to make a choice between dark and warm or the refrigerator, go with the fridge.

Buy cold-pressed olive oil. This means that heat has not been applied to extract the oil from the olive, so the taste is far more pure and intense.

There is a real difference between "olive oil" and extra-virgin olive oil. *Extra-virgin* means the oil is the product of the very first press-ing of the olives; it simply tastes better than any subsequent pressing, which will contain less actual olive taste and more of the bitter pomace taste of the olive pit and skins. That bitter taste is oleic acid, released as the olive oil is broken down by pressing. Crude pomace oil is not edible, but olive-pomace oil is great for cooking (see below).

For most of the recipes in this book, use a moderately-priced extra-virgin olive oil and buy it in larger quantities. In cooking, it will make all the difference (see Spaghettini Aglio e Olio, page 123).

Parmigiano-Reggiano

This is the king of cheeses. Its name comes from Parma and Reggio-Emilia, but it is also produced in Modena and parts of Bologna. The cheese was made with skimmed cow's milk and processed according to the highest standards and very specific rules. They don't take cheese lightly in Emilia-Romagna, lucky for the rest of us. One of the great things about Parmigiano-Reggiano is the fact that it doesn't go bad; in fact, it gets better and better the longer you have it, so don't bother buying one labeled *stra vecchio*, which is "extra old" and has a very strong taste that is overpowering in most applications. Instead, get a big hunk of Parmigiano that has been aged for a year or two and keep it, wrapped tightly in plastic wrap and also inside a sealed container or Ziploc bag, in the fridge. It is best to grate your own cheese right when you need it, so avoid already grated Parmigiano. At home, I like to put a big hunk of Parmigiano and a grater right on the table when friends come over. If, however, the only version of the real thing you can find is grated in advance, choose that over imitation Parmigiano. It really doesn't substitute, so no green bottled parm dust!

The way to make sure you are getting the real thing is to check that the rind of the cheese is stamped with the words *Parmigiano-Reggiano*, as in the photo. Although it can cost over twelve dollars per pound, I implore you, if you are going to skimp, don't do it here. A little goes a long way, and you will use every bit of it, including that rind, so don't throw it out (see Escarole Soup, page 107). If you buy a pound of Parmigiano-Reggiano, you will be set for quite a while. Considering that, it's a worthwhile investment in the good life.

Do not confuse Parmigiano-Reggiano with other grating cheeses, like pecorino or locatelli romano. Those are sheep's cheeses and have an entirely different taste. There are some dishes that could be served with either one, if you happen to like the more tangy, piquant taste of the sheep's milk, like Farfalle with Grilled Sausage, Fennel, and Baby Artichokes (see page 125). Pecorino is less expensive, but it should not generally be used instead of Parmigiano.

Tomatoes

Unfortunately, the climate in most of this country does not lend itself to lots of good fresh tomatoes. A lot of tomatoes are shipped from the West Coast to the East and are picked when they are still hard, so they will hold up traveling. The sacrifice is taste, so I eat and cook with fresh tomatoes only when they are in season in New York, and I urge you to enjoy the best local tomatoes all summer wherever you live. The rest of the time, canned tomatoes are truly great for cooking, whether storebought or, even better, canned at home. I grew up with the Labor Day weekend tradition of canning the tomatoes my grandmother grew on Long Island. My cousins, siblings, and I loved to help her with this process. To this day, my aunt Elena grows and cans whole plum tomatoes and tomato purée, and then uses them all year round.

Because we lived in Queens and didn't have our own garden, my mom used regular canned tomatoes from the store, as I do unless Elena has recently bestowed hers on me. The best canned tomatoes are whole, peeled San Marzano (a region, not a brand name) plum tomatoes imported from Italy. Don't let them fool you with cans of "plum shaped" tomatoes. Plum tomatoes are the sweetest and have the most taste, especially from San Marzano. However, when I bought some for my mother, thinking it would be a great treat, she scoffed at me for trying to improve something that was already perfect; she swears by Red Pack tomato purée.

Tomato purée can come from any kind of tomato (usually a combination) and generally has a less sweet, more watery taste than whole or crushed tomatoes. I still like my fancy tomatoes, especially for chunky sauces, but the ideal pantry should be stocked with whole peeled plum tomatoes, puréed tomatoes, and tomato paste.

Tomato paste is an Italian-American staple, although it is used in Italy as well. It gained indispensability here because American tomatoes are usually less sweet than Italian ones, and the paste, which should be used in small amounts, adds that sweetness back and thickens the sauce. Buy it in a tube if you can find it, or buy a small can and transfer it to a plastic or glass container as soon as you open it. Keep it in the fridge.

Olive-Pomace Oil

Use pomace oil or an olive oil blend for any dish in which oil serves a cooking function but is not ultimately part of the finished product. It is made from the pits of olives and is somewhat cloudy, which should not alarm you. It will impart a mild taste of olive oil, especially when it is cooked for a significant period of time. If it tastes bitter, blend it with canola oil or olive oil. A good rule for when to use different oils is simply to use the good stuff for short cooking times, the best

for dressing salads, or for drizzling over finished dishes, and pomace oil for searing sausages (see Rigatoni al Ragù, page 120) or any time the fat will be discarded.

Canola ~ Olive Oil Blend

Don't use pure extra-virgin olive oil for deep-frying, and not just because it's a waste of money. Olive oil has a lower smoking point than canola or vegetable, which means that by the time you get your oil really hot, you risk the oil burning, creating a bitter taste. However, to get the olive taste into your food, rather than just plain canola oil, use a canola/olive oil blend. You will be able to get it very hot, and you will taste the difference. Some supermarkets carry already blended oil, but you can easily make it by using 2/3 canola oil and 1/3 extra-virgin olive oil.

Red Wine Vinegar

When red wine sits around for too long to taste good, Italians add the culture that makes it into vinegar. Well, nowadays, of course, they make the vinegar outright, but the tradition was to keep a chain going in the house, adding wine whenever it was otherwise going to be thrown away. The older the vinegar is the better it tastes, but you will not be missing out if you buy regular inexpensive grocery-store red wine vinegar. If you are watching your budget, this is one place to skimp without really suffering.

Wine for Cooking

In Italian cooking, water and wine make up most of the liquid used. Most Italians, especially in Southern Italy, don't spend their time making stocks; in terms of having plenty of liquid, flavor, and acidity for braising (see Braised Short Ribs Pizzaiola, page 186), wine is the best choice. My aunts use white wine almost exclusively, regardless of whether they are cooking a whole rabbit or a whole snapper, but I think it's a personal preference, and you can decide depending on the dish and your mood. I generally use red wine if I'm cooking red meat and it's wintertime, but white if I am cooking chicken or rabbit in the summer, or fish anytime.

Lemons

Life in Italy does not exist without lemons. Lemons of all shapes and sizes are a food icon, as essential as salt and pepper. They work great with fruit, vegetables, seafood, fried food, and even steak (see Porterhouse and Potatoes Alla Mama, page 184). Wedges of lemon are often put out on a dinner table without a specific use in mind, but as go-to, default seasoning for anything. Lemon, olive oil, salt, and pepper are the classic combination for cooked vegetables.

Parsley

Italians use the phrase "Essere come prezzemolo," which means "To be like parsley," to describe something or someone ubiquitous. And it's true. Parsley is in almost every dish my mother makes. Italians use it to freshen their breath, to add texture to finished dishes, to make things look beautiful, and above all, for the taste. It also grows everywhere in Italy. Don't ever buy curly American parsley again. There is no point. Italian flat-leaf parsley is easy to find and has a really earthy, green, versatile taste. It's not sweet or too bitter, and it is the centering point of many recipes in this book. Although it is so common, it really pulls together almost anything. I appreciate it most in the simplest things. Sprinkling a little chopped parsley on plain scrambled eggs, for example, makes them suddenly taste grown-up, and turns pasta with butter and Parmigiano-Reggiano into a meal.

Basil

Adding basil to a dish is like adding sugar; it provides a bright, sweet, slightly cool anise-like flavor, and even the smell of it is powerful. I associate it with summer, since we only ate it fresh in my house. It gives me great joy that it can be found all year round now. Dried basil doesn't hold its flavor very well at all; the best way to preserve the taste is in canned tomatoes or, briefly, in oil. When you garnish a dish with basil, tear the leaves with your hands rather than chop them, because the basil will react with the metal knife and discolor.

Oregano

This is the quintessential Italian-American herb. Without the distinct taste of oregano, which most often comes from its dried incarnation, a dish doesn't quite register as Italian-American. It has a pinelike taste, and a smell that seems earthy and medicinal. In Southern Italy, oregano grows wild everywhere; it is harvested and used fresh but also dried and used in marinades, salad dressings, and sauces. Rosemary, another hearty herb to keep dried in the pantry if you can't find the fresh stuff, has a woodsy taste like oregano, but it is really a Tuscan, not a Southern, staple. If you love oregano, see page 84 (Clams Oreganata). If you hate it (as does my mother, shockingly enough), experiment with rosemary or thyme in its place.

Onions

Onions are great chameleons. Depending on how they are treated, they can be bitter and crunchy or soft and sweet, and they are used in most Italian dishes. My mother keeps regular yellow onions or big Spanish onions in her pantry all the time. I think red ones are great raw in salads or on sandwiches. They lend sweetness to dishes when they are "sweated," which is, along with garlic, the base of many recipes in this book. Sweating means slowly drawing out moisture. Simply chop onions and heat them in olive oil over a very low flame.

The onions will not gain any brown color—if they do, the heat is too high. They should, instead, become very soft and translucent. Adding a sprinkle of salt will speed up the process. This is the best way to start a sauce, because the liquid will flavor it throughout.

Garlic

When I was a kid, I thought garlic was simply decor, because it hung, braided, everywhere in my house and in my grandmother's. I had no idea it was food until I was about five years old. I vividly remember seeing my grandmother, while making eggs for me, reach up and break off a piece of garlic. I was shocked, thinking, had she lost her mind? She had destroyed a beautiful ornament. When I saw her smash it and throw it in a pan, it blew my mind. In this country, we can buy garlic whenever we need it; it does not decorate our houses. It is harvested in the spring, and if you can find it then, spring garlic is incredibly delicate and mild, even raw.

At Rocco's 22nd, the kitchen staff refers to "Mama garlic" often when talking about how to prepare dishes. It's our way of describing my mom's classic garlic treatment. She smashes each clove with the side of a knife, by pushing down on the knife with the heel of her hand. The skin comes right off. Then she trims any rough ends and throws it in a skillet with hot olive oil. While the garlic browns over medium heat, she smashes it further with the edge of a wooden spoon. I can't recall having ever seen her chop or slice it. Her method is easy, but it's also ingenious. All the tasty oils go right onto the pan and into the olive oil, rather than wasting away on a cutting board.

Anchovies in Oil

Fresh anchovies are one of life's great pleasures. Because they have a short season and are hard to find fresh, the preserved version you can find in the grocery store is the next best thing. Italians, like all Mediterranean people, preserve them in salt and then in olive oil. They heighten the briny seawater taste in any seafood dish and are really glorified in Linguine Puttanesca (see page 138) and Caesar Salad (see page 206). I know a lot of people think they don't like them and will take them off their plates if they are whole, but they melt away into sauces and leave a salty, ocean flavor without that intense fish taste. Surprisingly, anchovies and lamb have a serious love affair going on (see Baby Lamb Chops Scottaditto, page 174).

Mozzarella

Americans adore mozzarella, but the mozzarella we love is very different, especially in texture, from the original. In Southern Italy, mozzarella is made from water buffalo's milk. It is a lot wetter, creamier, and tangier. Mozzarella made in the States is much denser and drier. Hence, it has become, almost exclusively, a melting cheese. That's why dishes like parmigiana (see pages 162–167) became so ubiquitous here. If you can find fresh mozzarella, which should always come packed in cloudy water, eat it at room temperature with good tomatoes and a little of your best olive oil. Otherwise, start kneading your pizza dough (see pages 208-217).

Prosciutto

This is the cured leg of a pig, or, to Americans, ham. Never, ever, ask for the fat to be trimmed off prosciutto when you're buying it, I beg you. There is simply nothing like a paper-thin slice of prosciutto melting in your mouth, and the fat is really the whole point. It literally pains me to hear people ask for the fat to be trimmed off. They might as well skip it. Italians have mastered the art of curing, drying, and aging meat. Of all the incredible things they do, prosciutto from Parma is, without question, the best cured meat on the planet. Although this did not originate in Southern Italy, my family and Italian-Americans as a whole love it, especially with melon in the summer.

My rule is to keep it simple. Serve prosciutto all alone or on a plate with cheese, on a piece of buttered bread. In my family, it was eaten only on special occasions; my favorite way was with figs. I never cook with it, except to use the very end, which can be treated like a ham hock.

Make sure it is sliced ultrathin. The Italians invented a machine just to achieve the thinnest possible slices of prosciutto; it is powered by hand, because they realized that a motor-powered machine would heat up the prosciutto and melt the fat. That's devotion, and I urge you to, maybe less obsessively, make it part of your life, too.

Soppressata

Soppressata is the basic, inexpensive snack food of Southern Italy. It is salted ground pork, usually with whole peppercorns mixed in. It is put under pressure, which is what its name means. In the process, it dries out and shrinks. This is a type of salumi but not actually salami, which comes from the North and is made with very finely ground pork, so the fat and lean meat are totally integrated. I prefer the chunky contrast in soppressata.

Bread Crumbs

Bread crumbs are one of the best examples of peasant frugality. Bread is a big part of life in Italy, and when it gets a little too dry to eat, it is not discarded. In fact, I remember, when I was 11 years old, I threw out the dried end of a loaf of bread, and my grandmother slapped me, then dug into the trash to retrieve it, and slipped it into her apron pocket. She said something like: "Bread is life. Don't throw life away." Bread crumbs are used for breading fried food, thickening sauces and soups, adding a crunchy texture to sautéed or baked dishes, and binding stuffings. If you eat enough bread that you can make bread crumbs and keep them in the pantry all the time, that's great. When the bread is too old to eat, put it in a plastic container with holes in it so it can dry out, then break it up in the food processor to make fine ones, or with a mallet for coarse crumbs. Add a little salt, pepper, and oregano. But even my family buys theirs, because bread crumbs, originally just scraps, have evolved into an ingredient high in demand. Experiment with seasoned Italian ones. Usually, I like to add my own seasoning to plain ones. My mom uses Progresso.

Bread

In Italy, bread was not something one picked up presliced and packaged at the store. A lot of effort went into each loaf. My grandmother harvested the wheat, brought it to a communal mill, brought home the flour, made the dough, then brought that to the communal oven. For me, there has always been one kind of bread, and that is the basic crusty peasant loaf my grandmother, mother, and aunts make (see recipe, page 217). The same recipe can be used with white or wheat flour, but I like the wheat. It's good for you and has so much more taste.

Dried Pasta

In your pantry there should always be dried pasta. If you make fresh pasta, you should use it within a day or two. To cover all the bases, so you can always whip up dinner without even going shopping, I recommend keeping spaghetti or spaghettini, penne or ziti, and rigatoni on hand. I like penne rigate, which has ridges like a ribbed sweater, so whatever sauce you toss it with clings in the grooves. Generally, short pastas go best with chunky sauces, and long with thinner sauces. Of course, you should keep on hand the ones your family eats the most.

Eggs

If you're crazy about eggs and have the outdoor space, keep a few chickens in a coop. It will change your life. Fresh eggs are some of my favorite childhood food memories. If that is going too far, do yourself a favor and buy the freshest eggs. If you can find organic, always buy them. Refrigeration of eggs is not necessary, or even recommended. Cooking with a room-temperature egg is much better. If you refrigerate your eggs, take them out well in advance of cooking them. You will see the difference. The practice of adding egg yolks at the last minute to thicken sauces and give them a creamy texture is often attributed to French cuisine, but it actually started in the Medici kitchens. (See Spaghetti Carbonara, page 119, and Baby Lamb Brodettato, page 175.)

Risotto

Risotto comes from the Po Valley. It is also called arborio rice. I like the Vialone Nano variety, which is known as the "chef's friend." It is harder to overcook because it is a slightly larger grain.

Eggplant

There are many kinds of eggplant, used differently in cuisines from all over the world. If you like it, experiment with different colors, shapes, and sizes. But for this book, large Italian eggplant is all you need, and it should be very easy to find. Look for smooth, firm, resistant skin. When you slice it, sprinkle both sides of each slice with salt and let it sit for a few minutes, ideally on a cookie rack. The salt will draw out extra moisture and reduce the bitter taste that eggplant can hold. It will also increase the flexibility of the eggplant, so this is particularly important in dishes like Eggplant Rollatini (see page 76). It can be grilled, fried, sautéed, or pickled. And it's a meaty vegetable, so it will take center stage if you have a vegetarian to feed.

Other Key Ingredients *for* Your Shelves

Balsamic Vinegar
White Wine Vinegar
Provolone
Fennel
Artichoke
Broccoli rabe
Escarole
Arugula
Zucchini/yellow squash
Bell peppers
Mushrooms
Figs
Olives
Chestnuts
Hazelnuts
Pimentos
Capers
Red pepper flakes
Black peppercorns
Kosher salt
Sea salt
Ricotta
Garlic powder
Onion powder
Chickpeas
White beans
Chicken stock (canned)
Polenta
Flour
Sugar

Equipment for the Italian-American Kitchen

Ricer
Sauté pans: small, large, nonstick, stainless
Cast-iron skillet
Grill pan
Grill basket
Cheese grater (box)
Paring knife
Strainers
Long slicer
Mandoline
Pasta pot
Pasta machine
Gelato machine
Candy thermometer (for frying)
Mallet
Roasting pan

Meatballs, p. 78

Combine all ingredients

Mix well

Heat marinara

Simmer meatballs

Bread, p. 217

Incorporate wet ingredients

Knead dough

Shape dough

Let dough rise

Ravioli

Space out the filling

Press the dough together

Cut the ravioli

Finished Ravioli

Sausages, p. 80

Butcher pork shoulder

Grind the meat

Season and mix

Stuff the sausages

Fresh Pasta, p. 134

Crack eggs into well

Knead dough

Shape dough in a ball

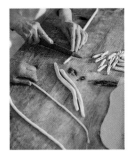
Shape the pasta

Mozzarella

Stretch the curd

Soften the curd

Braid the cheese

Finished Mozzarella

Grilling alle bracce, p. 185

Build wall of pit

Fill pit with wood chips

Start the fire

Let the flames die down

Butcher your meat

Place meat in basket

Hold baskets over embers

Grilled alle bracce

Epilogue

As a child I was uncomfortable with my ethnic background, but as an adult I embrace it 100 percent. My desire to open Rocco's 22nd Street was the ultimate manifestation of that pride. My mom and I poured our souls into it. She has been, and continues to be, the best partner I could have ever hoped for. The promise of a show on NBC primetime, a great location in New York City, and the help and support of all my relatives made us both believe that this restaurant would fulfill the dream of bringing the warmth of our home to the rest of the country. We had the time of our lives, and we hit some bumps in the road along the way. But the future is bright as ever. With the great support and energy we get from our fans, we intend to keep bringing the good life as we know it to all our loved ones, friends, and family for many years to come.

Index

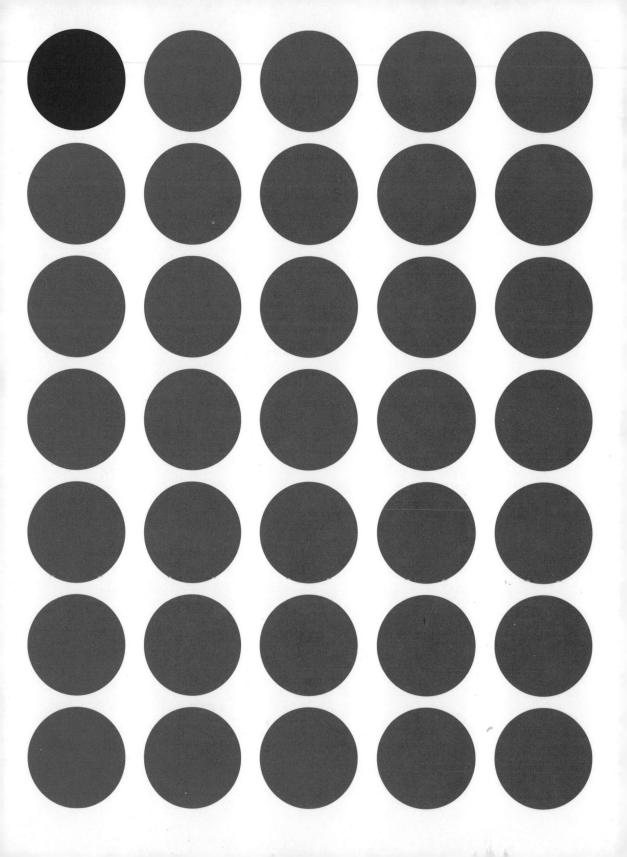